THE
HISTORY
OF
ROMSEY

A LTVAS Publication

Editor: Barbara Burbridge

River Test
viewed from the north-west
as it flows towards Romsey, seen in the middle distance
Photographed by David Young

The River Test was essential to the prosperity of Romsey from earliest times. It is thought, in fact, that the river's name dates back to the Iron Age, although it is only first found in writings of the 9th century. The earliest known spelling was 'Terstan'. So far, no satisfactory meaning of the name has been suggested.

CONTENTS

PREFACE

PART I

PART II

PART III

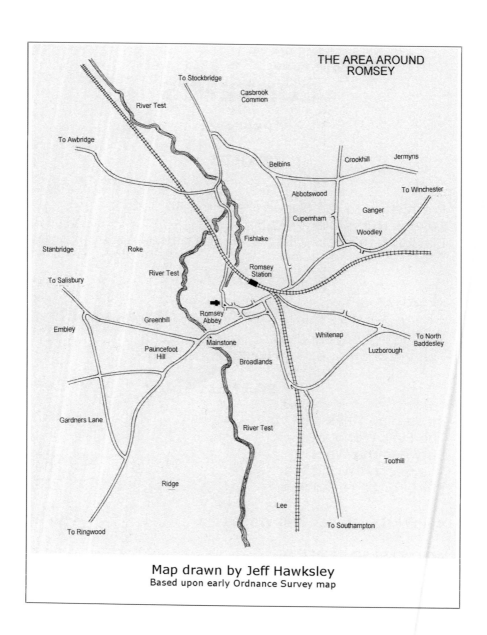

THE AREA AROUND ROMSEY

Map drawn by Jeff Hawksley
Based upon early Ordnance Survey map

PREFACE

Welcome to the story of Romsey, a small market town that evolved around a great Abbey. Its early economy was based on agriculture and milling, with emphasis on trades related to woollen-cloth and leather. In this, Romsey is representative of many similar-sized towns in the south of England, but has, besides, its own distinct geography and history.

This new book builds on our 1984 publication, now out of print, and incorporates much new research, as well as covering a greater length of time. We have looked back beyond the last ice age and brought the story of Romsey right up to the new Millennium. Inevitably, such a lengthy journey through time has necessitated much deliberation about what should be included or not, and doubtless some will regret certain omissions (especially about the times within living memory).

To give breathing space within an otherwise break-neck career through the centuries, we have paused now and then to look more closely at certain aspects of Romsey's history. These include the rural manors in the medieval period; Tudor life style as revealed by Romsey wills; the 18th-century poor; Victorian social life; and the 20th-century World Wars.

The overall result is very much the history of the town. Information about Broadlands and the Abbey - dealt with in admirable detail elsewhere - is only included inasmuch as it affected the town and its people.

We hope you will enjoy this new interpretation of Romsey's history alongside other more specialist books published by the LTVAS Group.

Barbara Burbridge
Pat Genge
Phoebe Merrick
and fellow contributors

Virgin and child
found during excavation in Romsey Abbey precinct, 1922
By kind permission of David Allen, curator of The Andover Museum

Part I

Prehistory

to

1550

Author/Co-ordinator
Phoebe Merrick

Photographic Work   Charles Burnett

Contributors
Steve Cooper, F.J. Green, John Papworth

The Local Terrain

As it approaches Romsey, the River Test leaves behind the chalk hills of the north and passes through gravel beds. The western side of the area is made up of a gravel ridge above the river valley. This ridge is fairly level and stands a mere 60 metres above sea level. The scarp face ends to the south of Romsey by Moorcourt where it is cut away by the river Blackwater, a tributary of the Test that joins the main river at Nursling. The slopes to the east of Romsey are gentler and lower than those on the west, being only about 50m above sea level.

The valley floor is low-lying and liable to flood. The most recent geological deposits are the brick-earths that overlay the gravels and the alluvium laid down as flood deposits of the River Test. At Romsey, a slight rise between the river and the eastern hills provided the focus for early settlements. To the south, again on marginally higher ground, lies the ancient hamlet of Ashfield, beyond which the hills reach a peak of 84 metres at Toothill.

The local soils are primarily dominated by the gravels albeit with some brick-earth, peat, and chalk deposits known as tufa. In places the peat achieves a considerable thickness, being more than five metres deep in the Greatbridge area.

PREHISTORY TO THE ROMANS

The Palaeolithic Period (Old Stone Age)
c500,000BC-c10,000BC

The earliest people to visit Romsey arrived thousands of years before the last great Ice Age, which finished around 10,000 BC. The River Test was a feature of the early landscape, and sometimes it carried great loads of gravel that spread on the land around Romsey, forming shelves and beaches. (The same action can be seen on a small scale in the Tadburn stream after it has flooded.) Like all rivers, it then cut through the gravel to form the river valley of today.

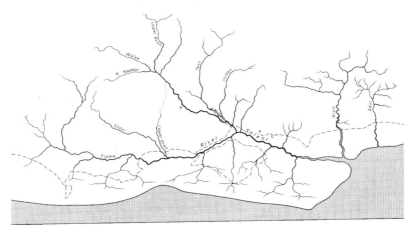

A suggested Palaeolithic coastline for central southern England
with the present coastline and the Isle of Wight indicated by dotted lines

The river valley was a good source of food, while the higher land offered drier and safer camp-sites. The first people were hunters and food-gatherers, and visited the low-lying river banks in their search for food and drink; but they would not have lingered in the floodland except in the kindest weather. Indeed, they led a nomadic life, never staying long in any one place, but nonetheless leaving evidence behind them. Moving around the landscape, as these nomads did, individuals dropped, lost or discarded items, leaving tantalising clues to their way of life.

Palaeolithic implements have been found in the gravels of the lower Test Valley. Some, showing signs of striation, were clearly washed down by the river, but others were found where they were made or used. On the valley floor, Palaeolithic flint implements have been found in the Latimer Street area of Romsey and near Lee to the south of Broadlands. On the high land, characteristically leaf-shaped hand axes and other flint tools have been found in the quarry at Ridge on the west, and flint tools were made in the Cupernham area, to the east of the town. The eastern hills have also produced finds at Ganger, Woodley, Whitenap and Luzborough.

Flint implements from Luzborough
Made available by Kay Ainsworth of Hampshire County Museum Services
Photographed by F.J. Green

As the climate fluctuated, groups came and went. In colder periods they would have left Britain, crossing the land link that still made it possible to retreat to mainland Europe. Sometimes, in less cold spells, they might return for summer seasons. Then, as the last Ice Age extended the fullness of its cold grip southwards, the area was uninhabited for several thousand years.

Mesolithic Period (Middle Stone Age)
c8500BC–c4000BC
The Ice Age ended; trees and plants grew, providing an environment for animals such as deer and wild pigs. Nomadic

people walked across from Europe, back into a land that was warming up. Then, as the ice retreated, the melting waters poured into the North Sea and inundated the land that joined Britain to Europe. In the Test Valley the river was gradually evolving so that, by the end of this middle stone age period, it was probably running on a similar course as now.

The tools of these nomadic people were identifiably different from those of the Palaeolithic era. Hand-axes were more elongated, and changes in hunting techniques required smaller flints in the tool kit - for this was the time when the bow was first developed.

The seasonal hunting camps of the Mesolithic people of the lower Test Valley have been found at Broom Hill (Braishfield), Abbotswood and Bowman's Farm (Ower). At Bowman's Farm, archaeologists have found shallow outlines, possibly indicating foundations for huts, and amongst the discarded tools was a small stone axe.

Closer to Romsey, another important find was a carved antler tine that had been dropped at the foot of Green Hill. This was carved from red deer bone, and was engraved with a pattern of chevrons commonly found on European Mesolithic artefacts. It is now in the British Museum.

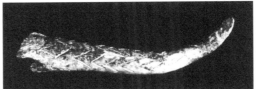

Antler tine found at foot of Green Hill
By courtesy of
the Trustees of the British Museum

Thus, from time to time, groups of Mesolithic hunter-gatherers came to the Romsey area, and crossed Green Hill and Ridge to the west or the swathe of high land running through Woodley, Halterworth and Luzborough to the east. From these moderate heights they would have seen the River Test on its course from the chalk hills of northern Hampshire, as it flowed through the valley floor between the hills, sometimes as one stream, sometimes as several, and, in wet weather, flooding much of the level ground.

Neolithic Period (New Stone Age)
c4000BC-c2500BC

The early Neolithic people were wanderers, as had been their forebears. However, the emphasis changed from hunter-gathering to management of resources. Initially, this applied only to cattle, which were herded and driven from one grazing site to another. Thus their way of life gradually changed and

with it their tools. Stone hand-axes became more sophisticated, reflecting widespread trade, and, for the first time, they made pottery vessels. Nationally, though not in the Romsey area, they built monuments and burial chambers and all these things mean that they left more remains than had their predecessors.

mace-head
found in Abbey Water
by permission of A. Feucks

Their movements brought some of them into the countryside of Romsey. A polished mace-head has been found in Abbey Water and part of an axe-head at Mainstone. Pottery from this period as well as stone axes, some polished, have been found by Middlebridge Street, and at Broadlands. The Cupernham area was much used by Neolithic people who found in its gravels flints that were suitable for converting into tools. Evidence of habitation has been found at Cupernham, Abbotswood, northwards across the Fairbourne stream at Crookhill, and around Jermyns Lane. The people who left these deposits only visited the area.

Evidence suggests that Neolithic people then became settled agriculturalists. At first, they may have stayed only long enough to raise a crop, but towards the end of the period they settled for longer spells, as the benefits of agriculture became more apparent. They were helped to make the change because the climate improved, bringing with it weather that was both warmer and drier than today.

Bronze Age
c2500BC-c800BC

Although the warm period lasted well into the Bronze Age, the first evidence of settlement on the valley floor dates from the later part of the period when the weather was turning colder and wetter. People settled along the banks of a major braid of the River Test that had forced a channel through the slightly raised gravel platform. This braid once ran along the western edge of the present Market Place, and southwards down the line of Bell Street. (The braid had become a small stream by the Middle Ages, when it was known as the Shitlake.) Settlers spread out westwards on the lower edge of the long, dry platform that forms the core of historic Romsey. Because of later activity, it is not clear whether the first people to live in this area settled for long periods or merely found the place convenient for occasional use.

Despite this period being called the Bronze Age, neither bronze nor copper remains have been found in the immediate area. Nevertheless, Bronze Age pottery, flint work, skull fragments and animal bones, including those of pig and beaver, have been found in the old river bed west of Bell Street, around Newton Lane and Narrow Lane, and further west still in the grounds of La Sagesse Convent. Beavers were valued for their pelts, so the Bronze Age people of Romsey may have worn beaver amongst other things.

Further evidence of wealth in the locality was found in the 19th century with the discovery near Wade Bridge, to the south of Romsey, of a gold torque. This was a very thin twisted bar slightly more than a metre in length. There were hooks at the end, and it was probably worn around someone's neck. Although it

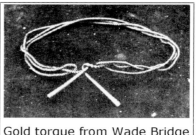
Gold torque from Wade Bridge

has since been lost, there is an electrotype copy in the British Museum.

In the latter years of the Bronze Age there was settlement at Luzborough to the south, where pottery of the period was found in the 19th century. At the time, the pottery was thought to come from burial urns, which may have been interred in round burial mounds. Amongst other things, a saddle quern has been

13

found at this location, showing that corn was being ground into flour at a place with a subsequent long reputation for corn growing. The meaning of Luzborough as a place name is difficult to understand, but may suggest the site of an early defended settlement. Pottery fragments suggest that some Bronze Age people lived at Great Woodley, as did others at Sandy Lane and at Gardeners Lane to the west of Romsey.

Towards the end of the Bronze Age, there seems to have been a greater use of hill-tops. It does appear that the wider Romsey landscape was becoming more intensively used during this time. At first there were only settlements, but some later developed as hill-forts. In the lower Test Valley, these hill-forts were of a different scale and size from well-known chalkland sites such as Danebury, near Stockbridge. More typical of the Romsey area were Lockerley Camp to the north and Toothill to the south. Although Toothill's 'fort' possibly belongs to the early Iron Age, spearheads found there were made in the Bronze Age. While major hill-forts such as Danebury clearly had a defensive role, the purpose of the smaller ones is not apparent.

Iron Age
c800BC-c100AD
The Iron Age opened in the cool, wet climate that had dogged the late Bronze Age. Gradually, bronze implements were overtaken by stronger tools made of iron. People made their way back to the lower ground, where settlements came and went. Much of the pottery found in the grounds of La Sagesse Convent was finely decorated and therefore of high status, suggesting that the area had become important. Furthermore, the discovery of loom weights indicates that weaving was undertaken there. And, as befits the Iron Age, part of the Newton Lane/Narrow Lane site was used for smelting iron in the later part of the period. So these people were not only farmers, but followed industrial pursuits as well.

Some people established their homes on a second 'island' plateau between Love Lane and Station Road. This was some way to the east of the Shitlake, which flowed between it and the Newton Lane settlement. Evidence of an Iron Age presence was unexpectedly discovered in the 1980s. In what was meant

14

to be a training excavation to give practice on techniques, a team of archaeologists found late Iron Age pottery, and three boundary ditches. They also found three small pits and post holes, offering clear evidence that people lived there during part of the later Iron Age.

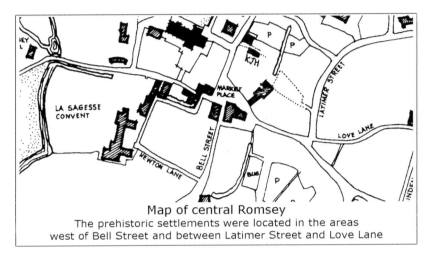

Map of central Romsey
The prehistoric settlements were located in the areas
west of Bell Street and between Latimer Street and Love Lane

Also on this eastern side of Romsey, but further south, there is evidence of sporadic use of the land between The Hundred and Broadwater Road, where botanical evidence and pottery have been found. The manure that was spread on these fields contained pottery sherds in amongst other rubbish.

The hills above Romsey were inhabited intermittently throughout the Iron Age. Farmers created terraced fields on the slopes of Toothill, giving rise to a 'Celtic field' system, and there are several ditches of the period in that vicinity. There may also have been a settlement on the western ridge in the Gardeners Lane area, and nearby on Green Hill postholes indicate a possible house site. Back on the lower ground, but north of Romsey, there were neighbours on Casbrook Common north of Timsbury Lake. The inhabitants of that site included weaving in their activities.

Two Iron Age gold coins have been found in Romsey. One of them is now in the British Museum. It is known as a stater and was found somewhere near the present railway line. The other gold coin was found over a century ago, possibly in the Station Road area. Like the gold torque, no one now knows where it is. More recently, an Iron Age silver coin was found in the Newton Lane area.

Coins are a helpful guide in defining how Romsey fitted into the large tribal units that were forming as the Roman threat materialised. At Nursling, Romsey's close neighbour to the south, almost 100 bronze, silver and gold coins have been found. Most of these coins were minted by the Durotringian tribe from the Dorset region, with some minted by the Atrebates to the east. This suggests that Romsey was on the border between the Atrebatic and Durotringian tribal centres.

It leaves open, however, the question of the political control of the area. The governance of all the diverse farms and semi-industrial settlements immediately in and around Romsey is not apparent. To date no high status Iron Age complex has been identified for such a role.

The Roman Period: c100AD–c410AD
There seems to have been re-occupation of the Newton Lane area west of the Shitlake before the Roman invasion by Emperor Vespasian, who was in command of the Roman Legions that conquered the area in and around Romsey. There are several Roman sites in the vicinity with villas at both Braishfield and Ampfield, possible small townships at Nursling and at Bossington (near Broughton to the north), and finds from Abbotswood, Cupernham, Timsbury and Carters Clay.

People continued to live to the west of Bell Street and across to La Sagesse Convent. They may not have been 'Romans' as such, but may well have been Romano-British people, descendants of Iron Age Britons who absorbed the life-style of the new conquerors so completely that they seemed like a different race. The transition may not have been rapid, though, and they probably lived in simple timber buildings during the 1st and 2nd centuries. At some point in the late 2nd century a ditch was dug across the site, probably to mark out a boundary. The pottery was not of the finest quality, suggesting local farmers rather than sophisticated villa dwellers. Nevertheless, the discovery of a stylus implies some level of literacy.

The site has been difficult to interpret archaeologically, but two coins found indicate occupation at each end of the Roman period. The first was a copy of a Claudian coin minted at the time of Nero (37-68AD) when there was a shortage of coins. The second, a coin of Gratian, belonged to the 4th century.

Roman material was re-used by later inhabitants of Romsey and has been found in other contexts. Roman tile, for example, has been found in the remains of furnaces built by Saxon iron smelters. Large decorated Roman stone was incorporated into the Saxon church that preceded the present Romsey Abbey, and has been discovered in the foundations that still survive.

People were living in the Station Road/Love Lane area in Roman times. In addition, others appear to have lived by Oxlease Farm at Cupernham during the 3rd and 4th centuries. There may also have been a small late-4th-century settlement in the area of the modern Romsey Industrial Estate behind the railway station.

These individual farms would not have existed in isolation, but there is real evidence to indicate a source of authority over the scattered homes. It is unlikely that there would have been any sort of military control. Romsey was in the peaceful settled area of Roman Britain, so there would have been little need for a military stronghold away from the coast.

Reconstruction of a Saxon iron-smelting kiln
By permission of F.J. Green
Iron-smelting was the first known large-scale industry in Romsey.
It lasted from the mid-7th century until the 10th century.

Early Industries of Romsey

A tenter-frame
By permission of The Museum of Welsh Life
Cloth-finishing dominated Romsey's urban economy throughout the monastic period. After woollen cloth had been fulled, it had to be stretched back to shape and size on frames, or racks, such as the one shown. Two old fields called Rack Close are known, one north of Mill Lane and the other west of Bell Street.

FROM THE SAXONS TO THE BLACK DEATH

People have been living in central Romsey continuously since about 700AD. A burial from that time was found inside the Abbey in 1839. Significantly, it was below the level of the first Saxon stone church. A lead coffin had been lined with oak: inside was an oak log used as a pillow, on which rested a plait of hair (now to be seen in a showcase in Romsey Abbey). Only someone very rich or powerful would have been buried so expensively, and the implication is that Romsey clearly had influential patronage in the pre-monastic period.

The Name of Romsey

The name of Romsey is a very ancient one. The 'ey' ending comes from an Old English word for an island - in this case an island surrounded by waterways and marshland. The meaning of the first part of the name is less easily interpreted, but is now thought to derive from the name of an important Saxon leader of the 9th century or earlier.

Originally, the name would have applied only to the settlement that developed on - and to the north and south of - the prime site where Romsey Abbey now stands.

Romsey's Iron Smelters

Some of the early Saxon inhabitants of Romsey made their livelihood by iron-smelting in the area west of Bell Street. They found low-grade iron ore in chunks of stone lying on the sandy soils to the west of the River Test and in the New Forest. Trees for making charcoal were plentiful all around. Thus, with the raw material and the fuel to hand, there was a basis for a local industry, which eventually spread over several acres. The smelters probably found customers at Hamwic (Saxon Southampton) or perhaps Winchester.

It is possible that they were under the protection of successive kings in Saxon times, when Romsey is thought to have been a royal estate. So the iron-smelting may have been an early example of royal commercial enterprise.

19

An Early Minster

Christianity was the established religion of the West Saxons from the mid-7th century onwards. During the late 7th and early 8th centuries, a network of minster churches was established in Wessex. These religious centres were set up in important locations within the kingdom, and covered a much wider area than the parishes of later times. Clergy based in a minster travelled around the area served by their church, taking the faith to the people. If, as has been suggested in recent years, a minster was established in Romsey, the king may have allowed the revenues of the iron-smelting as a financial support.

The Mid-Saxons in Romsey

It may be that royal interest in Romsey was not restricted to the central site. King Ethulwulf of the West Saxons was buried at a place called Stambridge, which could be modern Stanbridge Earls to the north of town. There is added justification for this idea from the fact that the king's descendants owned the adjacent areas of Embley and Michelmersh, and possibly Stanbridge itself, until the Norman Conquest. Furthermore, Ethulwulf's wife was a Frankish princess, Judith, who is said to have arranged for the remains of St Bathild to be interred at Romsey in the 850s.

> ### St Bathild
>
> Bathild had been an Anglo-Saxon slave girl in the kingdom of the Franks but married King Clovis II. She had three sons by him, the eldest of whom, Clotaire, was only five when his father died in 657. Bathild acted as regent, during which time she founded monasteries at Corbie and Chelles, and was active in suppressing the slave trade. She was removed from office in 665 in a palace revolution, and spent the rest of her life at Chelles as an ordinary nun. She died in 680 and her remains had been taken to Paris in 833.

These high status sites were not the only places where people were living in mid-Saxon Romsey. Separated by waterways and by a ditch that crossed The Hundred about 50 metres east of the Market Place, there was another smaller settlement north of Love Lane in much the same area as the occupation that had occurred in the Iron Age. This time it seems likely that blacksmiths were at work, because a large pit has been found with remnants of charcoal and smithing slag. The area has also yielded Saxon pottery sherds and rubbish.

South of the modern Hundred, in part of the land now occupied by car parks, was a field called Periton, a Saxon name meaning a place where pear trees grow. The Saxon farmers, however, seem to have grown wheat, barley, oats, rye, and peas and beans there. Remains of wild radish and hazelnuts have also been found in the Periton area, amongst other material.

The settlement in the Latimer Street and Love Lane area was cut off by another waterway that ran along Latimer Street (the name of which - Lortemere in early records - may mean slow-moving stream). This water then followed the line of The Hundred and Palmerston Street until it joined up with the Tadburn stream. There is no evidence about how people crossed Romsey's waterways in those early centuries.

Romsey Abbey
There is no record to show how the town of Romsey fared during the first wave of Viking raids that troubled southern England in the latter part of the 9th century. Alfred, the king who had had to deal with these incursions, left to his wife and daughters some estates that subsequently came to be owned by Romsey Abbey. These estates were at Edington in Wiltshire, Wellow and Clere in Hampshire and possibly Steeple Ashton in Wiltshire. There is thus a property link between Romsey Abbey and King Alfred.

Alfred died in 899, and popular tradition in Romsey is that the nunnery was founded in 907 with his granddaughter, Elfleda, daughter of Edward the Elder, serving as the first abbess. There is conjecture, though, that the foundation may be of earlier date, since the Abbess of Romsey also owned prestigious Winchester property that had been parcelled out by Alfred in 885. Whenever the actual foundation took place, a monastic house of nuns had certainly replaced any previous ecclesiastical establishment by the beginning of the 10th century. Some of their buildings had chalk foundations, suggesting something more substantial than mere timber-framed structures, and implying wealth and permanence.

The Rule of St Benedict

In 959, King Edgar came to the throne. Amongst other things, he presided over the monastic reform inspired by St Dunstan, then Archbishop of Canterbury, and Romsey was one of the establishments affected. The nunnery was re-organised, and the nuns undertook to follow the Rule of St Benedict, which provided for an orderly and balanced monastic life. One part of the rule involved work, and English nuns were renowned for their embroidery skills in Saxon and Norman times, though whether this was a pastime at Romsey is not recorded.

King Edgar granted the Romsey nunnery extensive lands on the eastern side of the River Test. These lands eventually evolved as Romsey Infra and the eastern part of Romsey Extra. They stretched northwards to Timsbury, eastwards to Ampfield woods, and southwards through part of modern North Baddesley and into the edge of Lordswood, before turning back towards the river past Grove Place at Nursling. The Abbey was clearly a very wealthy establishment because the nuns gave the king:

> 'a goblet of marvellous workmanship, handsomely chased armlets and a scabbard richly decorated with gold, together with 900 mancuses of pure gold'

These gifts were described as being in exchange for the woodland part of the grant. It was about this time that Edgar's young son, Edmund Atheling, died, and an old document refers to his being buried in 'the minster at Romsey'.

The 10th-Century Town

Hardly anything is known about the town of Romsey in the first half of the 10th century. Iron-smelting had declined and the one-time industrial area was partially given over to horticulture, but lay people were needed to support the hundred nuns permitted under the terms of Edgar's refoundation: so the population must have increased, though probably still only to be counted in hundreds. During this century, land to the north of the Abbey complex came into use. People started to live in the Church Street and Portersbridge Street areas.

At this time, there was farming in the area of New Road, Cupernham, and the spreading of rubbish there, which implies a nearby settlement. Place names also suggest that there were scattered farmsteads elsewhere in rural Romsey.

The Danish Raids at the First Millennium
All the wealth of the Abbey was not sufficient to protect Romsey from raids by Danes, who camped on the Isle of Wight and ravaged the south coast at the end of the 10th century. By this time, it is said, the nuns were seeking a new abbess after the death of the highly regarded Abbess Merwenna. In her place they proposed Elwina who, while at her prayers, received divine warning of raids. As a result the nuns had time to flee to the safety of Winchester, a fortified city. Nothing is known about the fate of the ordinary inhabitants and whether they also fled, or chose to remain in Romsey.

The nuns' flight took place around the year 1000. Within three years Elwina herself had died, and Ethelfleda, ward of King Edgar, was elected in her place. It was during her abbacy that the nuns were able to return to Romsey. This is the lady who became St Ethelfleda, to whom the Abbey church is jointly dedicated along with St Mary.

The 11th-Century Abbey
The returned nuns built a new church, and the stone remains of this building are still under the present much larger one. Two relics survive from the Saxon church. These are both roods depicting Christ on the cross. The large rood is outside, set into the west wall of the south transept, a location that was once sheltered within the cloisters. In recent years, it has been the subject of specialist work to preserve it from weather and damp. The small one is in St Anne's chapel of the present church: it has lost the gold and jewels with which it was once adorned. Both roods are fine pieces of work, and demonstrate the wealth of the Saxon Abbey.

The Beginning of the Norman Period
The coming of the Normans in 1066 did not change the status of the Abbey, which continued to be patronised by royalty, although its income was reduced. In 1086, William I ordered a national taxation survey, recorded in the famous Domesday Book. The Abbess is shown as holding Romsey and other places directly from the King as one of his tenants-in-chief.

The value of the Abbey's Romsey estate, as stated within the Domesday survey, had diminished by nearly one third between the 1050s and the 1080s. This may suggest that the Norman invasion had had its effect on the area.

The Domesday survey is the first document that refers to the inhabitants of Romsey as well as the nuns. The entry divides Romsey into three parts, two estates of unequal size where the land was let, and one that the Abbey retained as a home farm. On the larger of the rented estates there were 39 villeins, 53 lesser tenants and two slaves. The tenants had 16 ploughs between them and there were three mills worth 25s 0d in all. There were 50 acres of meadow land, and sufficient woodland for grazing 40 pigs. (This estate also included the Abbey's property in Winchester, where there were 14 tenants who paid 25s 0d.)

TERRA ÆCCLÆ DE ROMESYG.

.XV. Abbatia de Romesy ten tota uilla in qua fedet ipfa æccla
T.R.E. fe defd .p. xiiii . hid . Modo .p. x . hid . Tra . e . xviii . car.
In dnio funt . ii . car . 7 xxxix . uilli 7 liii . bord cu . xvi . car . Ibi . ii .
ferui . 7 iii . molini de . xxv . fol . 7 | xxx . vi . ac pti . Silua de xl . porc .
In Wintonia . xriii . burgfes . xxv . folid reddentes.
De hac tra ten Hunger . i . hid 7 una v . 7 iiii . alij libi hoes ten
ii . hid dimid v min . Ibi fuŋ in dnio . iiii . car . 7 xiii . bord 7 ii . ferui.
Tot T . R . E . ualb . xix . lib . 7 poft : fimilit . Modo : xxiiii . lib . qd
abbatiffa ten . Qd hoes : xl . fol .
Ipfa abbatia ten 7 tenuit una hida . ubi funt . iiii . uilli cu . i . car .
7 molin de . x . fol .   Val 7 ualuit . xx . fol .

Extract from the Romsey entry in Domesday Book

The smaller portion related to lands where there were five freemen of whom one was called Hunger, the first named inhabitant of Romsey. It also included 13 lesser tenants and two more slaves. This second settlement was not identified but it could have been in the Love Lane-Latimer Street area.

Finally, the home farm estate of the Abbey was valued at just 20s 0d. It contained one hide of land - perhaps 100 or so acres - on which there were four villagers and a mill worth 10s 0d. It has not been possible to determine where this estate lay.

The Domesday survey only listed Abbey tenants, and did not account for their households. In addition, there were lay servants within the Abbey, so the population must have been several times bigger than the Domesday total of some 114 Abbey tenants.

William I's great survey leaves gaps concerning the landholdings surrounding Romsey, especially on the west bank of the River Test. Before the Norman Conquest, Earl Godwin, father-in-law of Edward the Confessor and father of King Harold, had held Embley, Awbridge, Little Somborne and Chilworth. William I had awarded these lands to one of his supporters, Bernard Pancevolt, whose family gave their name to Pauncefoot Hill. However, there is no mention of Stanbridge, Roke or the lands around Green Hill and Pauncefoot Hill. It is likely that they also went to Pancevolt. Since the estate at Embley was deemed to have declined in value from 10s 0d to nothing, they were probably not considered worth mentioning.

The Abbey's Royal Connections

In the 1090s, one of the distinguished nuns of Romsey was Christina, a Saxon princess. Her sister Margaret, later canonised as St Margaret, married Malcolm III of Scotland (Malcolm Canmore of 'Macbeth' fame). Towards the end of the 11th century, Margaret and Malcolm sent their two daughters to England to be brought up under the supervision of their aunt. The elder daughter, variously known as Edith, Maud or Matilda, was courted by William II, the eldest son of William the Conqueror. Christina did not consider him a suitable match for her niece and put a nun's veil on her in order to persuade William that she was not available to be his wife. It is said that Christina took the king into her garden and showed him her roses, and if this is true it is the only time William Rufus seems to have shown any interest in women or roses. After his death in 1100, his brother succeeded to the throne of England as Henry I, and he also paid court to Matilda, although by then the family may have moved to Wilton nunnery.

Matilda's position as the potential mother of Saxon claimants to the throne made an alliance politically important. After it had been established that Matilda had not taken the veil, she was able to marry Henry. Like her mother, she engaged in many good works and was known as 'Good Queen Maud'.

During Matilda's lifetime, Henry visited Romsey in 1105 on his way to France, but there is no way of knowing whether his queen was with him. Henry granted various privileges to Romsey Abbey, including one allowing the holding of a four-day annual fair and a weekly Sunday market, in each case with rights to administer justice at those events. In his charter, Henry specifically granted these rights to the Abbey and to Matilda his wife; no mention is made of an abbess, so there may have been a vacancy with Matilda in nominal charge. In another grant, Henry allowed the Abbess to try cases of murder within historic Romsey Infra. Murder was the unlawful killing of Normans and not only was the offender hanged but his goods were liable to forfeit. There is no evidence that any abbess ever dealt with such a case.

Medieval Romsey Infra was small, lying between the Holbrook stream on the east and the River Test on the west. The Holbrook stream can be seen in the Lortemore Place car park near King John's House and by the side of the bus station. In medieval times it was crossed by a bridge at the end of the Market Place, known then as the Broad Bridge (and only later as the Hundred Bridge).

By 1120 the nuns had started to replace their Saxon church with a fine building in the Romanesque style. There is no evidence to show who paid for this expensive project, which took some 130 years, on and off, to complete. Perhaps the Abbey financed it by selling some property, or perhaps Henry I or Matilda, or both, gave money. There may even have been a connection with Matilda's death in 1118. Whatever the source of funding, the church is now one of the finest examples of Romanesque architecture in England because the Abbey never again had the money for a major rebuilding of its church. As the new church was built over the site of the old, the nuns would have suffered great inconvenience. For years, they must have felt that they were praying in a building site.

26

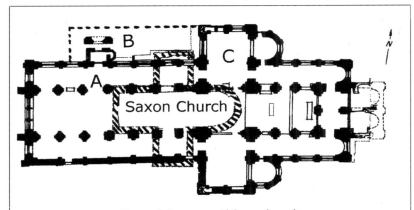

Plan of Romsey Abbey church

The outline of the much smaller stone Saxon church is shown within this plan of the present Abbey church

A = the north aisle, dedicated to St Laurence in medieval times, when it acted as the parish church

B = the approximate area of the early 15th-century extension to St Laurence's

C = the north transept which became the chancel of the parish church when the extension was built, and which is still dedicated to St Laurence

The nuns worshipped separately in the main body of the Abbey

Work started at the east end with stone from the royal quarry at Quarr on the Isle of Wight. As the builders worked their way back, they reached the apse of the old church, which was then demolished. The nuns then had to worship in the new choir, while the nave was completed behind them. Some parts of the west walls of the crossing and the transepts were built from poorer quality Bembridge stone, also from the Isle of Wight. There is no record about how the stones were transported. In the 13th century, Chilmark stone from Wiltshire was used on the final phases of the west end, and these must have come by cart, heavy loads customarily drawn by teams of oxen.

The fact that Romsey Abbey continued to attract adherents of the highest social status is shown by the presence of another princess who was Abbess in the 12th century. This was Mary of Blois, the youngest daughter of King Stephen and therefore cousin of Henry II who succeeded Stephen. She was dedicated to the monastic life when very young, and became Abbess of Romsey in 1155, when she was only about 19 years old. Within five years, her brother William, Count of Boulogne, had died, leaving her as heiress to extensive lands in France. This estate was too important to be left leaderless, and Henry II arranged for Mary to leave the Abbey and marry Matthew of Alsace. Mary did not wish to marry, and the affair scandalised the whole of Europe, including Matthew's parents and the Pope. The marriage lasted ten years, after which Mary ceded her lands to Matthew and withdrew to a nunnery in France.

The last known example of a princess coming to live in Romsey took place early in the 13th century, when King John sent his daughter, Joanna, to live in Romsey and be educated by the nuns while she grew up. She did not live in the Abbey but in a house that her father had built somewhere in Romsey, and which his son Henry III later granted to the Abbey. Henry himself visited the Abbey in 1231 and gave it five oaks from Melchet Forest for the repair of the dormitories. Forty years on, his son, Edward I, gave six oaks from Clarendon Forest for the rebuilding of the Lady Chapel, and visited Romsey three years later. Despite these gifts, there were no more long-term associations with royalty after Princess Joanna.

Nevertheless, the Abbey continued to attract high-born ladies throughout the 13th century. Amongst such were Abbess Matilda Patriz and Abbess Alice Walerand, both descendants of Walerand the Hunter, a prominent landholder in the Domesday survey. Many Walerands occupied high office until the male line died out with the death of Alice's brother Robert in 1272. Perhaps the most illustrious name of this century was that of Abbess Isabella de Neville, who came from the influential Neville family; a later member of this family, Anne Neville, would become the wife of Richard III in the 15th century.

The Election of an Abbess
The election of a new abbess was an important event. First, the death of the previous abbess was reported formally to the king, sometimes personally by the nuns themselves, and licence to elect was sought. During a vacancy, the possessions and incomes of the Abbey were taken into royal custody and administered by an escheator. These officials did not always

have an abbey's interests at heart, and abbeys often paid a fine to the king in order to keep affairs in their own hands. Between the abbacies of Matilda Patriz, who died in 1230, and Matilda de Barbeflet, who was elected in 1231, the affairs of Romsey Abbey were put into the hands of Walter de Romsey, the Abbey's steward or seneschal.

The nuns were free to elect whom they wished, although the Bishop of Winchester might choose to be present at the election. In addition, three prebendaries were entitled to vote in the election. These prebendaries were priests whose income derived from the revenues of Romsey Abbey and who occupied prebendal stalls in the choir of the church. Their role within the Abbey is not clear, and the posts seem to have been largely sinecures by the 13th century. Even though the nuns, as women, could not undertake priestly duties themselves, the prebendaries did not conduct services for them: the nuns had to employ other clerics. If there had been an early minster before the nunnery was founded, these prebendal offices may have survived from that period of Romsey's history.

The nuns usually chose an abbess whose name would carry prestige in society; social links were often considered more important than either spirituality or administrative capability. After being notified of the election, the king would restore all the incomes or 'temporalities', which were vital to running such an institution.

Abbey Finances
Although Romsey Abbey possessed great wealth, it was not all at the disposal of the nuns. As well as supporting the prebendaries and priests, the nuns needed to pay their lay employees from the Abbey Steward downwards. They also had a continuing obligation to provide £20 worth of alms for the support of 20 old and feeble men and women, as stipulated by King Edgar in his charter, and there were other charges upon them.

The nuns were grateful, therefore, for any donations that added to their income, but the days of receiving great estates yielding valuable revenue were gone. In the 13th century, their wealthy supporters offered lesser gifts. At the end of the 1200s they were given a house and land in Itchenstoke, house and land in Repling (which cannot be identified) and a house in Romsey. Walter le Flemyng, a prominent Southampton merchant, left just £1 to the Abbey in 1258. By this time the rich were more inclined to arrange endowments, so that masses could be said for their souls and those of their families. For example, in 1244, Joan Neville gave about 100 acres of land to the church on condition that the Abbess found a suitable chaplain to undertake such duties for ever.

The Braishfield Chantry
During the 1330s, a notable endowment of this conditional nature was made to the Abbey by a wealthy local couple, Nicholas de Braishfield and his wife Emma. They endowed a chantry within the Abbey church. Nicholas had been an important person in Romsey for many years, his name appearing as a witness to legal documents as early as 1307. In 1331, he granted the Abbess a house and 25 acres of land in Romsey, but with the proviso that, out of the income, the nuns undertook to find a chaplain to celebrate, or chant, divine service daily in the Abbey church for the souls of Nicholas and his wife. This chantry grant was re-inforced in the following year by the gift of further lands.

Also in 1331 Nicholas became Abbey Porter, a prestigious position, akin to head of security, with underlings to carry out the day-to-day duties. As Porter, he received substantial daily rations for himself and a servant, as well as 5s 0d annually for a robe and bran for his horse. It is tempting to link the appointment as Porter with the establishment of the chantry. If there was such a link, then it continued after 1335, by which time Nicholas was dead. In her widowhood, Emma granted to the Abbey another six properties with 60 acres of land, 13½ acres of meadow and 34s 11d of rent in Romsey, although she retained use of them for the rest of her life.

Bishops' Visitations
The Abbey was still highly regarded in the 14th century, though the high social status of the abbesses did not necessarily mean that they always behaved as they should. One of the duties of a medieval bishop was to visit the monastic establishments in his diocese and to check that all was well. After a 'visitation',

he would write to the house about those matters that needed attention. By modern standards, it was a very bad management style, because no credit was given for what was done well; nor was reference made to previous visits. Each report stands on its own as a list of shortcomings, which can make the unwary reader think that all medieval monasteries were dens of iniquity.

There is no evidence that the 13th-century Romsey Abbey was morally degraded, although there clearly were problems from time to time. For example, in 1283, Alice Walerand was instructed not to appoint servants without consulting the other nuns, and she was not to entertain guests after compline (evening prayers) had been said. It would seem that she was living finely and entertaining at the expense of the other nuns.

The Abbess and the Town
The administration of market and town continued to be in the hands of the Abbey. A wide range of responsibilities and privileges lay with the Abbess as lord of the two manors of Romsey. There was, however, a distinction between the manors in terms of the level of authority enjoyed by the Abbess.

In respect of Romsey Extra the Abbess answered to the county subdivision known as the Hundred of King's Somborne, as was normal for rural manors, but within Romsey Infra the Abbess had her own court with hundredal powers, augmented by privileges granted by Henry I. In respect of Romsey Infra, she was answerable directly to the king's county sheriff and to no lesser official.

The Abbess appointed a Steward and other lay officials to administer her manors. Through the Steward and his underlings, the Abbess administered the town's annual fairs as well as the weekly market. Amongst the many lesser town officials, there were those responsible for the assise of bread and ale, an early form of quality control. Many households relied on bought bread and ale, as they lacked the facilities to make their own. The Abbess appointed aletasters to oversee standards and to bring to the manor courts those brewers and bakers whose goods were below standard. At one time, the

Abbess's right to do this was challenged in the royal court but was upheld by reference to one of the charters granted by Henry I.

13th-Century Romsey: Rural and Urban
It is from the 13th century onwards that the town of Romsey and its inhabitants really come into focus. The names of parts of 13th-century Romsey and its surrounding manors appear in surviving documents, particularly those held by Winchester College, which once owned considerable property in the area.

Approaching the town of Romsey from the west, the obvious way to cross the River Test is over Middlebridge. But there is no record to show when it was built. King Edgar's 10th-century charter makes no reference to such a bridge, as might be expected if it had existed then. However, it must have been built by the reign of Edward I (1272-1307). From that time there are several surviving documents that feature properties in Middlebridge Street, which obviously took its name from the bridge. During the reign of Edward I, for example, Gilbert le Gold sold to Robert le Gold, his son, a tenement in Middlebridge Street for £2.

The Three Tuns, Middlebridge Street, with the turning into Eny Street on right

Before Middlebridge was built, travellers leaving town followed the line of modern Middlebridge Street only as far as the entrance to the *Three Tuns* car park. There they turned south down a road called Eny Street and crossed the Test somewhere south of Romsey. Once the Middlebridge crossing was available, travellers preferred it, and Eny Street was used much less. It still continued in existence, but was down-graded as Eny Lane; its path could be traced until the late 18th century, after which it was absorbed into Broadlands Park.

Other street names that can be dated back to the 13th century include Bannock Street (later Banning Street), Cherville Street, Churchegatestrete (a possible early name for Church Street), Latimer Street and Porters Lane (later Portersbridge Street). There are also various references to pieces of land or shops in Romsey Market, or sometimes more specifically in the 'shoe market', the 'fleshshambles' or the 'Shambles'. Whether these specialist areas were within the larger market space or at separate locations is not known. Some properties are simply described as being 'outside Broad bridge', meaning beyond the bridge at the east end of the market place.

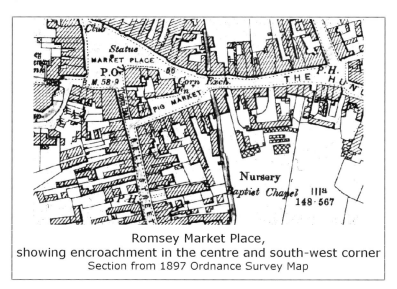

Romsey Market Place,
showing encroachment in the centre and south-west corner
Section from 1897 Ordnance Survey Map

These names show how the street pattern of historic Romsey was evolving in the 13th century. The Abbey church was dominant with the adjacent monastic precinct secluded behind stone walls. The wall on the town side featured an imposing gateway onto the market place. In front of the wall ran a stream over which the Abbess gradually allowed buildings to encroach. The market place, controlled by the Abbey Steward, lay to the east of both wall and stream, and was bounded at the east end by the Holbrook stream. This focus of Abbey precinct and market place dictated the flow of streets in and around the developing town.

33

The market place and the streets, although within a recognisable framework, would have looked vastly different from today. Buildings were less closely packed than they are now. Street frontages were gradually filled up, but side entrances remained to allow for the delivery and storage of animals and goods at the back of the property. Most buildings were houses and workshops combined where craftsmen both made and sold their wares. Some occupations required considerable space; the butchers' quarter or shambles, for example, must have filled a large area especially as butchers used the streets for preparing meat.

Romsey People

As well as streets, the names of some Romsey inhabitants emerge from 13th-century documents. Apart from the freeman simply called Hunger in the Domesday survey, the earliest names of ordinary people date from this time. Amongst them was a Ralph Hunger who in 1200 lived in Latimer Street.

It is not apparent how cosmopolitan medieval Romsey was. For example, the only trace of a Jewish community in Romsey occurs in 1263 when a royal order was made banishing Jews. This was at the request of Robert Walerand, perhaps as part of the general persecution of Jews in England during the middle of the 13th century. Only five years later, Alice Walerand became Abbess, so he had family connections with the Abbey.

The oldest surviving property deed with names in it was written in 1228, when Robert of Depeden [Dibden] and Edith his wife granted a house in Romsey, with two acres of land and a field, to Walter, son of Roger. Sadly, there is no clue as to the location of this house and lands. Two years later, in 1230, there was a land sale that involved Eudo of Aumbley [possibly Embley] and a certain Richard, the father of Alina, her husband Robert Turgis and her sister Matilda. The next person to be named appeared in a very different context. Andrew Turnecutel was accused of robbery and the Sheriff of Hampshire was ordered to take him to London.

Others also behaved in an undesirable way. The records of the New Forest Courts, sometimes held in Romsey, reveal that men of Romsey, usually in gangs, were from time to time accused of poaching. In 1250, for example, Henry Pistor and Richard Faber were each fined 2s 0d for poaching and William Bovedon 1s 0d. Some time later, in 1286, a group broke into the Bishop of Winchester's park at Merdon, near Hursley, and did much damage. The Bishop 'in great wrath' wrote a formal complaint to the Abbess, asking her to prevent a repetition. In 1297, two people were appointed by the king to find out who had assaulted Almericus de Sumersete in the woods at Romsey. Whether they were successful is not recorded.

On a more respectable note, Thomas le Nugg bought a plot of land near the water and bridge at Banning Street around the 1250s. He had permission to build on the site - just 32ft x 10ft narrowing to 7ft - as long as he did not impede the flow of the water, though the name of the stream was not given.

A more prominent person was Alexander le Dyer, whose name was sometimes Latinised as Alexander Tinctor. He lived at the very end of the 13th century and into the next, and held properties in Cherville Street and Portersbridge Street and two acres of land in the common fields known as Street Mead. His wife, Christina, and daughter, Ethelfleda, were well provided for. Alexander was probably a dyer by trade, and his Portersbridge property alongside the Holbrook would have been a splendid location for a dye workshop. It is tempting to think that Alexander bought dyestuffs from Thomas de Foxcotte who was allowed to burn beech and other trees in the New Forest in order to make potash for dyeing cloth.

Henry, son of Robert Carter, probably a carter by trade, sold a house in Churchgate Street for 26 marks, only just over £17 but a sign of a valuable piece of real estate for the time. His affluence may have derived from the building of the west end of Romsey Abbey and the need for supplies to be brought to the church. Afterwards, there was further work when the cloisters were built against the south side of the nave.

It was at this time, too, that someone of wealth and power built a stone house on a substantial site in Church Street. Perhaps from the beginning, and certainly within the high medieval period, it was roofed with the pinkish Devon slate that was favoured by the few who could afford it. This prestigious property - still surviving and mistakenly known today as *King John's House* - was probably the only stone building outside the monastic precinct. Its original purpose can no longer be determined but it appears to have played a formal role of some sort. Even if not built for the Abbey, it came into the Abbey's possession at some point.

Agricultural Romsey

Although Romsey had an identity of its own and an industrial economy, it must never be forgotten that it was a small town, and much of the population was directly dependent on agriculture. Many of the place-names of rural Romsey that survive today were common in medieval documents. Documents, and the discovery of medieval pottery, endorse the fact that Lee, a present-day hamlet to the south of Broadlands, was settled in medieval times.

Yokesford, Abbotswood, Woodley, Halterworth, Whitenap, Luzborough and Ashfield were all to be found, though the spellings might vary. Whitenap, for instance, has evolved from Whytenharpe or Whythernape, and the original meaning is in some doubt. Luzborough was sometimes called Lushborough, and Little Luzborough was spelt 'Inlilusborough'.

The town of Romsey, bounded by the River Test on the west, was surrounded to the north, east and south by agricultural land, much of it owned by the Abbey, some of it long established as common fields. Other areas had been enclosed as plots known as closes or crofts. Even people with industrial or commercial interests held strips of arable or meadow land in these common fields.

One area of meadow was in Street Mead which is now the site of Budds Lane industrial estate at the northern end of town. It lies close to the main waterways, as did the other meadow lands of Romsey, such as the Fishlake Meadows to the east of Street Mead and Mill Lane to its south. These common meadows were divided into strips, and parcelled out in half-acre lots. They provided the hay that was so essential for the winter feed of animals. One of the meadows reached from Mill Lane was called Gallows Mead, which may relate to the right of the Abbess to erect a gallows. Mill Lane itself was important, not only as a way to the meadows but also because it led to the corn and fulling mills that stood on the major off-shoots of the River Test to the north of the lane. These were later known as Burnt Mill, Mead Mill and Test Mill.

The main grazing land - the manorial waste - was to the east of town, uphill from Cupernham Lane, and encompassed the Abbotswood area. Manorial tenants were able to pasture their animals there on payment of fees. There was also some arable land in the area, as is shown in a 1374 sale by Robert le Cook to John le Forester. Cook sold four acres in Cupernham in a croft called Goycroft or Goyscroft. This field name has been lost since its last known use in 1427.

The main arable fields, growing corn and pulses, were to the south of the town with the uplands at Whitenap and Luzborough being particularly good for corn crops. Broadlands - or 'Brode Lands' - belonged to the Abbey in medieval times, and included other common fields, named East Grove, Chasletts and Emmetts, and Austrey.

Close to the river at the western edge of Broadlands, there were more meadows. Nearby, Waldrons Bridge - on a site now within Broadlands Park and long gone - led to the few town lands west of the river.

The Countryside Estates in the 14th Century
The Abbess did not own all the lands of Romsey. In particular, those parts of Romsey to the west of the River Test were mostly held by other landowners, as separate manors, although they lay within the parish of Romsey. There are references to these estates in 1242, when Mainstone just beyond Middlebridge, Spursholt at the top of Green Hill and Stanbridge were all mentioned in an official document. This document provides the first ever mention of Mainstone and Spursholt and the first reference to Stanbridge in about two hundred years.

In 1261 or thereabouts, a dispute about the pasturing of animals at Ridge came to court at Westminster. The result was that Hugh de Hoynill was fined for overstocking the common land at Ridge, above Pauncefoot Hill, and in future he was restricted to pasturing a maximum of eight cattle - oxen, cows or heifers - six pigs and twenty sheep.

From the 14th century, there is more evidence about the estates surrounding Romsey. In 1315, there was a dispute about lands in southern Romsey between Richard, son of Nicholas de Barbeflet, and a group of men supporting a certain John Moudenard. Moudenard had tried to take possession of lands that Richard de Barbeflet held in the Wools, Woobury, Ashfield, Woodley, More and Little More districts of Romsey Extra. The lands involved were probably those of the manor of Wells, all or part of which came to be called South Wells. This dispute was between men of substance. The Barbeflet family, for instance, were lords of the manors of Shirley and of Wells, and Matilda de Barbeflet had become Abbess of Romsey between 1231 and 1237. Amongst Moudenard's supporters were Sir Walter Escudamore, and John and Peter Escudamore whose family gave their name to Skidmore in Nursling. Another of his supporters, John Uphull, was also a man of repute, for ten years later he was prepositus, or reeve, of Romsey.

Close to Skidmore, but across the river, lies Moorcourt. In the middle ages Moorcourt was subdivided into More and Little More - or More Abbess and More Malwyn. More Abbess seems to have been some of the few Abbey lands immediately to the west of the River Test, although in 1367 the Abbess was given More Malwyn by William Malwyn and his wife Joan.

In 1316 a list of estates was produced, in preparation for taxation of landlords by the king. It includes many place-names that are now considered to be within the town of Romsey, but were once separate hamlets dotted around the urban centre.

There is still a fairly dispersed settlement at Ashfield, on the Southampton road beyond the end of the 'Mile Wall' around Broadlands Park. Its most conspicuous feature today is Ashfield roundabout at the junction of the A27 and the A3057.

Neither Embley nor Roke were mentioned in this list, though Roke may have been included in Stanbridge. It is noticeable that Stanbridge was held by two men, which implies that it was divided by the end of the 13th century. This may have been the origin of the north/south split later known as Stanbridge Earls and Stanbridge Ranvilles, which names have survived into modern times. Stanbridge Earls house is now a school, and Stanbridge Ranvilles survives as Ranvilles Farm which lies back from the south side of the A3090 above Pauncefoot Hill.

Romsey Area in 1316

Place	Held by
Borough of Romsey	Abbess of Romsey
Hamlets described as settlements	
Cupernham	Abbess of Romsey
Halterworth	Abbess of Romsey
Whytenharpe	Abbess of Romsey
Asshefelde (Ashfield)	Abbess of Romsey
Wopbury	Abbess of Romsey
Lec (Lee)	Abbess of Romsey
Welles (Skidmore area)	Abbess of Romsey
Marstone (Mainstone)	John Pauncefoot
Purshete (Spursholt)	Ralph of Monte Hermery
Stanbrigge (Stanbridge)	Thomas Danvers and Richard Portesey

The 14th-Century Town

With the opening decades of the 14th century, more of the town streets emerge from the shadows. The market area became more clearly defined as permanent buildings replaced market stalls around its edges. Building was taking place on the west side of Church Street and the Market Place, both beside and across the stream that backed on to the Abbey wall. Recently, archaeological evidence has revealed possible 14th-century structures within No 2 Church Street.

There was an active property market in Romsey, and other buildings around the Market Place were being bought and sold. For example, in 1314, Amice de la Chamber, a widow, sold a tenement in Romsey market to William atte Hoke for the sum of 20 marks (£13 6s 8d), and this tenement was described as being between the tenements of John Walston and Nicholas le Gonetir.

Nicholas Gonetir also leased another tenement in 1317. It contained 'a hall, a shop next the street with a room over it, part of the stable as far as the partition, a plot between hall and stable'. The property was a combination of home and workplace where the shop was a workshop and not merely a retail outlet.

Intriguingly, a street called Millbridge Street appears in documents from 1300 to 1330, after which it disappears as a name. Fortunately, at least one Millbridge Street property was thereafter described as being in Mill Street - so it seems likely that the earlier name was shortened. It would have been a sensible change in order to avoid confusion between Millbridge Street and Middlebridge Street. As Mill Street was the early name for Bell Street, and was the highway linking the Market Place with Middlebridge Street, the need for clarity is obvious.

There was, indeed, a Mill Bridge at the south end of Mill(bridge) Street. It crossed the Holbrook into Banning Street at the point where Broadwater Road now leads out of Bell Street. The mill bridge was over the part of the Holbrook that formed the tail race emerging from the Town Mill, which once filled the site of the present *Duke's Mill Shopping Precinct*. This mill belonged to the Abbess of Romsey Abbey, and this may be the mill at which all her tenants were required to have their corn ground.

The 'Spittle' or Hospital of St Mary Magdalene and St Anthony, first recorded in the 1330s, provided shelter for lepers and paupers. It was safely away from the urban centre, and was probably on the south side of Winchester Road, more or less under the railway embankment by Botley Road. This hospital was reached from the town centre by Spittle Street, which lay in the general direction of The Hundred. People who wanted to go to Winchester would not have used Spittle Street but would have travelled up Latimer Street and across to Cupernham and then continuing eastwards via the Braishfield area.

North from the Market Place, Church Street (as opposed to Churchgate Street) features in documents from the early 1300s. The street became popular with a number of clerics, and other high status individuals. The Abbey clergymen, not being allowed to sleep within the monastic precinct, had houses in this and various other parts of Romsey, as is reflected in property deeds. Such men sometimes acted as trustees in property deals for other people.

By the 14th century the town seems to have been divided into administrative areas known as tythings. Romsey Infra had three tythings, with the Market Place tything being the most affluent at the centre. To the south was Middlebridge tything and to the north, Cherville tything. This last tything probably encompassed one of the newer parts of town, for it is thought that Cherville Street was developed as a planned settlement in the earlier part of the 13th century. It was long associated with the manor of Rockbourne, near Fordingbridge, and the link between the two may have been the 13th-century Walter de Romsey. He was an important landowner with possessions in Somerset, Wiltshire and Hampshire, where he was lord of the manor of Rockbourne, as well as serving as the Abbey Steward. A very wealthy man, he was well able to invest in a planned housing development like many great landowners of his time.

Trade and Industry

Evidence of both tanning and the finishing of woollen-cloth, together with many related trades, can be found by the beginning of the 14th century. Together, they were the town's two chief industrial activities during medieval times and beyond. A range of documents record the names of individual tradesmen by the beginning of the 14th century.

For example, in 1307, William Imber, a fuller, bought land in the town. Fullers pounded woollen cloth in a solution of fuller's earth until the cloth was clean and the fibres felted together. They then stretched, or racked, it to restore shape and to avoid matting. Once dry, other craftsmen brushed the cloth with teasels, and skilfully cut off the loose fibres with shears to create a nap.

A teasel, growing in King John's Garden Summer 2000

41

In earlier times fulling was carried out by people known as 'walkers' treading the cloth in fulling pits. Later, however, it was realised that the power of watermills could be harnessed to drive great fulling stocks, or hammers, to do the work of men's feet. Water power became all-important, and Romsey was strategically placed to become an important cloth-finishing centre on a commercial scale. The gentle water of Romsey's waterways was an added bonus for this work, and was also very suitable for the allied trade of cloth-dyeing, which in time also became a significant part of the local economy.

Any spinning and weaving in Romsey seems to have been on a much smaller scale. During the 13th century some weavers made small coarse cloths called burels. The men who made these cloths were called tapeners. One such was Robert Tapener who had a property, described as being by Banning Street and 42 feet long by 8-9 feet wide. The tapeners' trade seems to have died out before the Black Death.

Tanning lasted in Romsey until the 20th century, though it never reached the affluent heights of the cloth-finishing industry. Three tanners are known from the early 14th century, when they were involved in land transactions. They were William Gille who bought premises in Mainstone in 1307; Walter the tanner who bought land near Middlebridge, also in 1307; and John the tanner, who, in 1325, bought a house in Millbridge Street.

It is noticeable that these men all worked in the southern end of Romsey, where the water was flowing away from the town. Tanning has always been a notoriously anti-social occupation, with many noxious smells and pollutants. It was preferable, therefore, to site it where it would cause least nuisance, though in the case of Romsey the prevailing winds would have subjected the inhabitants to many days of unpleasant odours.

People such as Walter the tanner and John the tanner did not always have established surnames but were referred to by their craft. Another man so named was John the tailor who lived in Newton Street (later Newton Lane) and was witness to a deed in 1329. Some years later there was a tailor known as Robert Scissor.

There were some very well-to-do people living in or around Romsey by the first half of the 14th century. In 1339, King Edward III forced people to sell him their wool with the promise that he would pay for it once he had sold it in Flanders, hopefully at a profit. In fact the debts were not repaid for some years. Only substantial owners of wool were involved, and amongst the Romsey men who were obliged to make these loans were Andrew Parlebien and John Bach. The first was owed £4 6s 5d for 371 pounds of wool and the second was owed £4 10s 1¾d for 469 pounds of wool. These amounts of money represent the pay of a skilled artisan for perhaps six to eight months.

In the national archives is a 1340 list of those Romsey people affluent enough to be liable to pay a tax known as a subsidy. It records that 72 local people were liable for a total payment of £8 13s 4d. This is a smaller number of people than those on the list of Abbey tenants in the Domesday survey, but only people of substance paid this tax, and clergymen were taxed separately.

The individual amounts varied from 2d owed by Robert Soylde to 6s 0d each to be paid by James Hayward, William Gille (the tanner) and Adam atte Burgg of Romsey Infra and John Webb in Romsey Extra. Some women were included, but they would have been widows. Amongst those named were Agnes Gobet, Christine Poun and Margery Uppehull in Romsey Infra and Isolda atte Corner and Margery Webb in Romsey Extra.

The Black Death, 1349
As the 14th century began, the Abbess continued to exercise her power as lord of the manor, but the fortunes of town and Abbey were no longer quite so interrelated. Although Romsey remained subservient to the Abbey, the town's increasing industrialisation was already weakening the old relationship.

The Abbey was changing too. The nunnery was declining in both social status and in academic standing, although the presence of 91 nuns shows that the community still had power to attract postulants. The nuns, unlike their Saxon predecessors, no longer had a competent grasp of Latin. They were still from good families, since amongst themselves they used French, which was the language used by the upper classes throughout the Norman period and well into the 14th century. The names of the nuns present in 1333 suggest that some were still from noble families, although others were of local gentry origin with surnames derived from Hampshire place names such as Ropley, Breamore, Winchester, or Hamble.

The Black Death came to Romsey in 1349, and brought about catastrophically a decline that might otherwise have taken place more gradually. The Abbess, Joan Icthe, died, and so did at least one of the prebendaries, Richard de Lusteshull, and two vicars, Nicholas de Botelston and William de Bures, the latter just two months after his appointment. No doubt many of the nuns also succumbed, for there were never more than 25 nuns thereafter.

Nothing is known of how this dreadful plague affected the townspeople, but it must have dealt a severe blow to a small town as it did throughout England and Europe.

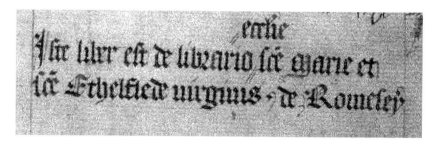

The title page of a book from Romsey Abbey
(discussed on page 46)

Hic liber est de librario ecclesie Sancte Marie et
Sancte Ethelflede virginis de Romesey
This book is from the library of the church of St Mary and
St Ethelfleda the virgin of Romsey

FROM THE BLACK DEATH TO THE DISSOLUTION

The Abbey: Aftermath of the Black Death

The Black Death hastened a downward trend in the Abbey's fortunes. Economically, the nunnery was already in a parlous condition, partly blamed on royal taxation and 'other burdens' which had caused the Abbey to be 'depressed by the burden of poverty and misery'. Then, after the plague had passed, the nuns had to adapt to the loss of their Abbess, many of their own number and several of their priests and officials.

As they attempted to resume normality, this loss of leadership, together with their poor academic skills, left them very vulnerable. Plague deaths amongst their estate workers, on whose efforts their income depended, would have depleted the Abbey's coffers even more. In the short term, the Abbey was reduced to penury, and the nuns to begging in the streets.

Rescue came from William of Edington, Bishop of Winchester. In a series of settlements, he received Abbey lands at Edington, Wiltshire, where he subsequently founded a priory, in exchange for Romsey properties that were more immediately useful to the nuns. These new properties cannot now be identified but they were in the possession of a man called John le Rede. They included 6 houses, 52½ acres of land, 12½ acres of meadow, 2 acres of moor and 69s 11d rent in Romsey. In addition, when the leases terminated, the nuns were to receive 12 more houses, 12 acres of land and 4 acres of meadow, all from named tenants. The Abbey Steward who negotiated on behalf of the Abbess was Roger de Haywode, who had been Steward in the 1340s - so he, at least, had survived the Black Death.

Beyond the Black Death

In the longer term the Abbey was affected by changing attitudes in the second half of the 14th century. It became less common for women to 'take the veil' as nuns, and less socially acceptable for women to receive an academic education. So the nuns were both of lower social status and, though cultured, they were largely uneducated. Romsey Abbey still attracted novices from the families of the county gentry, but not from the great families of aristocratic England.

Nuns from lesser families brought smaller dowries than those of aristocratic girls. New endowments to the abbey were further depleted by the continuing shift towards chantry endowments rather than straightforward bequests to the nunnery. There were still welcome exceptions of gifts from local gentry and Abbey officers, though, as may have been the case with Nicholas de Braishfield in the 1330s, some of these may have been a cover for the sale of its offices by the Abbey. In 1353, Roger de Haywode, the Steward, granted messuages, rents and lands. Amongst a group of donations made in 1367 was one from William de Putton, then the Steward, and another from Richard Pauncefoot, who subsequently became Steward in 1371. Whatever machinations may have been employed, the Abbey's income seems to have dropped compared with earlier times, while outgoings continued. New prebendaries and other priests had to be appointed, and their livelihoods funded.

Field names still suggest how revenue from specific Abbey lands helped to support both clerical and lay officials of the nunnery. Priestlands (where The Romsey School now stands west of Greatbridge Road) and Steward's Land (now the sports fields south-west of the Southampton Road roundabout) are two such places. Abbotswood was sometimes written 'Abbeiswood' thus reflecting its ownership by the Abbey.

As well as those holding high status positions, the Abbey still required basic administrative officials. Scribes would have been needed in the scriptorium, where writing was undertaken for practical matters, such as accounts, and perhaps also for more spiritual purposes. One of the British Museum's 14th-century treasures is a book of the lives of Anglo-Saxon saints that may have been written in Romsey. Experts say that the handwriting is that of an East Anglian scribe, but the first page states that the book is from the library of the church of St Mary and St Ethelfleda of Romsey. The saints whose lives are described include Ethelfleda, Merwenna, and Bathild who are all particularly associated with Romsey. The book is well written and many of the capital letters are in colour. Maybe the scribe originated from East Anglia but worked at Romsey.

Quite apart from clerics and lay officials, the Abbey employed many domestic servants, since it was not considered appropriate for nuns to attend to their own domestic needs. Indeed, there were times when bishops, making their periodic visitations of inspection, ordered them to reduce the number of servants, and to manage them better. Bishops also occasionally complained about little boys in the nuns' dormitory, and children being taken to night services. Despite their own lower educational standards, the nuns still seem to have augmented their incomes through teaching or perhaps childminding. What they were able to impart to their pupils other than lessons in manners is not apparent.

Abbey Finance
The 1412 Abbey accounts survive, and present a fascinating picture of a community failing to live within its means. The total income for the year was £404 6s 0½d, being the revenues from estates in Romsey, elsewhere in Hampshire and in Wiltshire. The expenses, unfortunately, were greater than the income, being in excess of £430. Some of the outgoings arose because of the need to repair buildings on their various estates.

Other details reveal the Abbey's sense of priorities. The highest sum, £110 6s 8d, was devoted to the personal and private household expenses of the Abbess herself, which sum did not include the shoeing of her horses, or hiring horses on her behalf and sending messengers on her business; nor did it include wine for visiting nobles. While the Bishop of Winchester was given a gift of £10 on his return from the Holy Land, alms for the poor amounted to only £8 19s 4d.

Charity
There is no mention in the 1412 accounts of the leper hospital or the Abbey charity set up by King Edgar; so the financing of these institutions is not apparent from this source. Nevertheless, the Abbey must have continued to honour its obligation to provide for 20 poor and old people, as had been required by King Edgar, because records show the custom continuing in the following centuries. Whatever the state of their own finances, the nuns were still expected to follow the charitable philosophy of St Benedict.

The leper hospital along Spittle Street was a refuge for lepers and probably also for people with other poorly diagnosed skin

...eases. All were treated as if they were as contagious as the true leper, and therefore isolated. Since the poor were also received at this hospital, it was in great demand and had been in need of alms even before the Black Death.

In 1317 and 1331 royal protection had been granted to successive hospital proctors, as they travelled to seek alms for the institution. The first of these two proctors was identified only as John, the second as Alan Unwyn. The second grant followed within two weeks of a visit to Romsey of Edward III, but it is impossible to tell whether there was a connection. It is equally difficult to decide whether the visitation of the plague some 18 years later left in its wake a greater or lesser need for the hospital's services and the Abbey's financial support.

Abbey Complex
By the early 15th century the whole monastic precinct had developed, and few innovations were made in the final century of its existence, when the buildings served no more than a handful of nuns. This was the Abbey's least active period, with the extensive building of earlier times completed, and only repairs or minor works taking place.

The gateway continued to dominate Romsey Market Place and much of the Abbey complex was surrounded by a wall. From the north-west corner of the church, the wall extended westwards and then turned to enclose the nuns' community area to the south before returning back to the north-east corner. It was probably primarily made of flint but whether it was completely continuous is not known; there may have been gaps where protection from the outside world was not thought necessary. Outside the east and south walls ran the stream that now flows under the shops in the Market Place, and surfaces in Abbey Water; it would have been necessary to cross this waterway to reach the outer courtyard of the Abbey that was encountered within the gateway.

Most of the church was used by the nuns for their religious purposes, although part was set aside for the townspeople. In addition, the Abbess had her own chapel, and there was a chapel of St Peter that may have been attached to the infirmary.

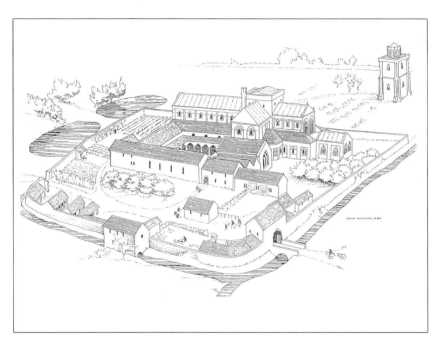

Reconstruction Drawing of Romsey Abbey, c1500

showing how the gateway from the courtyard of the Abbey precinct led into the Market Place, which was under the control of the Abbess by virtue of royal charters. The parish belfry is to the north of the Abbey church.

NOTE: This interpretation of the Abbey precinct was drawn in 1989, when it accurately represented the thinking of the time; it is a fascinating illustration of the continuing development of historical understanding. Further research since then has suggested the need for some amendments. Most notably, the mill that is shown over the waterway on the southern boundary cannot be traced further back than 1551 after the Abbey convent had closed. Its presence before that date must therefore be open to doubt.

The chapter house, the nuns' meeting place, was alongside the outermost wall of the south transept as was customary. In the area bounded by this transept and the south nave aisle lay the cloisters. These were roofed over to provide a covered walkway with an open space in the middle. There was a stone bench along the walls, where the nuns could sit. The corbels that supported the roof of the cloisters may still be seen protruding from the church's outer wall.

As in all Benedictine monasteries, the subsidiary buildings of the monastic precinct lay on the warmer, south side of the church. These comprised a range of buildings where the nuns and their household lived. Although men, including their priests, were obliged to have their homes outside the walled enclave, some of the Abbey's servants would have lived within the precinct.

Some parts of the domestic buildings still stand, concealed under later structures. About twenty-five years ago, for example, Numbers 13 and 15 The Abbey were found to contain medieval elements, believed to be the remains of the Abbey frater or refectory.

West of the River Test

Although the Abbey was the principal landowner in the area, there were other owners of substantial estates on the outer edges of modern Romsey. With the exception of the manor of South Wells, their lands and properties lay to the west of the River Test, an area that had received little mention in the Domesday survey, and where the Abbess had but one small holding. These lay landholders were wealthy gentlemen and some were socially equal to, or even superior to, the Abbess. Certain members of these families played their part in both local and national affairs. As well as administering their estates, they acted as town officials, or as royal servants, such as tax-gatherers.

Stanbridge Earls and Stanbridge Ranvilles

The most northerly estate in western Romsey was Stanbridge Earls. In 1361, Stanbridge Earls consisted of a substantial house, a watermill (probably Greatbridge Mill), 23 acres of arable land, and 3 acres of meadow. Associated with this holding was other land in the Romsey area, including a number of properties in Romsey town that brought in 100s 0d rent each year. In 1369, the then owner, Thomas de Overton, died at the age of 27, leaving a pregnant wife. A baby son was born, called Michael, and he was 17 years old when his mother died in 1387. Michael, as a minor, was a royal ward, and the King appointed men to administer the estates. Then Michael died just two years after his mother. He left a wife but no children, and his estates passed to his cousin, Elizabeth, wife of Robert Tauk. It has been suggested that part of the present house, now used as a school, could date back to the 14th century, when the de Overton family owned it, but this has not been confirmed.

In 1329, the separated southern portion of Stanbridge, known as Stanbridge Ranvilles, was held by Richard Ranville who was still there in 1346. Richard Ranville was a man of considerable standing. He was one of the men called to give evidence about the amount of wool, corn and sheep that could be paid as a tax by the parish of Romsey in one of Edward III's less successful money raising schemes. Whether Richard gave his name to the Stanbridge Ranvilles or took his name from it is uncertain.

Stanbridge Ranvilles is now bisected by the A3090, which makes it difficult to realise how it once spread from Spursholt southward to Ridge and beyond. Ridge seems always to have been a part of Stanbridge Ranvilles and not to have had a separate existence of its own. In later centuries, the land became part of the manor of Little Testwood, leaving only a farm to bear the name of Stanbridge Ranvilles.

Roke
Roke is probably a very old settlement but elusive in the records, perhaps because it was often linked with neighbouring Stanbridge. In 1347, a rent payment of 6s 8d went from Roke and Stanbridge to the estate of Hugh de Audeley, Earl of Gloucester. At that time Roke was known as Oke, and sometimes it has been called 'Quercus', the Latin for oak. Tantalising archaeological evidence indicates a deserted medieval village near Roke manor house, while several field names that include the word 'Park' suggest that there was once a medieval deer park in the vicinity.

Spursholt

Spursholt is also elusive and hard to trace. Even today the house is discreetly hidden from passers-by on the A27 to Whiteparish, and most people do not even realise it is there, let alone that it has medieval antecedents. In the 14th century, the area was known as Pershute, a name that is thought to come from the Old English meaning 'a pear-tree nook'.

In 1361, Peter de Pershute died and an account was taken of his lands. His estate at Spursholt ranked as a manor and comprised a house with a garden, 80 acres of arable land, 21 acres of meadow, 20 acres of pasture, a fishery, 12 acres of wood, free tenants paying rent of £2 yearly, and a manorial court that brought him 6d yearly. A Nicholas Pershute inherited the manor, but at his death in 1376 the estate was substantially less than it had been. The fate of the 'missing' acres is not apparent from the surviving documents. In 1361, part of Spursholt was occupied by William de Overton, as a tenant for life of Queen Philippa, the wife of Edward III. These lands consisted of a small house, 40 acres of arable land, 4 acres of meadow and 8 acres of wood, and was deemed to be part of the manor of East Tytherley.

Pauncefoot

Pauncefoot Hill
now a dual carriage way

Not all the lands of the western estates were confined to the hills above the river. Parts of Stanbridge Earls came down to the Test, and there was a fishery attached to Spursholt. South of Spursholt, built into the hill, stands Pauncefoot House. In the medieval period the Pauncefoot family, descendants of the Bernard Pancevolt who had followed William the Conqueror to England, held extensive estates in southern England. Their Romsey lands spread down the hill from Pauncefoot House to encompass Mainstone, the settlement on the west side of

52

Middlebridge. In 1316, this settlement had been called Marstone and was owned by John Pauncefoot. Apart from the house and outbuildings, there is little evidence of building on the hill, and it has not been established whether there was once a settlement there as well as the house. The Pauncefoots were probably the foremost family to have holdings of any size in Romsey, and their names frequently appeared as witnesses to deeds during the 13th and 14th centuries.

Moorcourt

South of Pauncefoot, beyond the present agricultural lands, lies Moorcourt where the scarp slope of the hills finishes and the river Blackwater cuts its way through from the west. Little is known about this area, but the name 'More' or later 'Moor' suggests swampy wet lands, good for reeds or grazing but not for arable use.

Wells

The name Wells has been lost in the last two centuries but was important for a long time before that. The extent of medieval Wells is difficult to determine, because there are early references to Wells, North Wells and South Wells. The most enduring name was South Wells, and this estate encompassed much land to the south of Broadlands.

From 1295 until 1329 the Wells estate was in the hands of the de Barbeflet family. Nicholas de Barbeflet, a rich Southampton man, held the estate from the Abbess of Romsey at a rent of 57s 4¾d, together with 2,000 herrings, 300 eels, ploughing 14 acres of her land and mowing 2 acres of her meadow. It was after this that the estate was settled upon John Escudamore, whose name evolved into the present-day Skidmore.

For several centuries the estate was linked with a number of people who had the surname Wells or Well. The importance of the family was again reflected by the frequency with which members acted as witnesses to deeds. Quite often the Wells name came first in the list of witnesses, a sign of social status, and when it did not, there is little doubt about the standing of the names that preceded it. The Pauncefoots, for example, ranked above the Wells, as did the Pershutes of Spursholt, but Nicholas de Braishfield ranked below.

Henry de Wells, who died in 1352, also had lands at 'la Wade', which is just over the river Blackwater by Wade Bridge. Later, at least, there was also town property, comprising three tenements on the east side of Church Street where Abbey Walk now stands. These premises were part of the South Wells estate for several centuries. The Wells family had also owned a house in Banning Street which Hawysia, widow of Walter de Wells, sold at the end of the 13th century. Banning Street would have been a convenient location for the family, since it was on the way south out of town, giving easy access to South Wells.

By 1472, the Abbey had lost its claim to the manor which then belonged to Thomas Greenfield whose family had held it for some time. Greenfield then resorted to some very dubious practices, selling the manor first to his brother-in-law, John Hamond and then almost immediately to the Duke of Gloucester. Subsequently, the Duke of Gloucester presented the entire manor to St George's Chapel, Windsor, who retained it for the next 400 years.

The Cloth-Finishing Industry
After the plague years, the emphasis within the town shifted from agriculture to industry, although agriculture was always important. With the expansion of the English cloth trade, Romsey fullers and dyers prospered during the later years of the 14th century and throughout the 15th century, and Romsey developed as an industrial town. The town became wealthy by finishing woven cloth; commercial weaving was not important locally at that time.

As early as the 1350s Romsey rated a mention in a document about the collection of customs duties relating to cloth. Men were appointed for these duties:

> in the port of Southampton, and all places thence to Portsmouth on the one side, and there, and in the Isle of Wight, and to Weymouth on the other side, and there and in the cities of Winchester and Salisbury and the town of Romsey.

No evidence exists of their activity in Romsey, but the very fact that the town needed to be named is an indication that its importance was recognised. It was at this time that Romsey traders became liable for a specific cloth tax called ulnage.

Ulnage was a new form of tax, first granted to Edward III by Parliament in 1353. It only applied to expensive woollen cloths that were for sale, and it was paid once the cloths had been fulled and racked. In Hampshire, the greatest number of payers of the ulnage was to be found in Winchester, but the second most important place, albeit a long way behind, was Romsey.

It is only in the 1390s, though, that there is evidence to reveal the true extent of Romsey's flourishing cloth trade. By then, Romsey tradesmen were mostly processing cloths called 'dozens', which were about 12 yards long and 45 inches wide. A list of the men of Romsey who paid the ulnage between 1394 and 1395 has survived and shows that some individuals were responsible for many more cloths than others.

Cloth Financiers

The people who paid the ulnage had not necessarily carried out all the manufacturing processes themselves. They may not even have financed them from start to finish but they were the owners of the cloth when the tax became due, and so it is their names that are recorded. Evidence from Winchester and elsewhere shows that some people with money to spare invested it in the production of high quality cloth.

Sometimes the local gentry became involved in trading but their status did not keep them out of trouble. In 1490, the Sheriffs of Wiltshire, London, Middlesex and Berkshire, but not Hampshire, were ordered to arrest Reynold Kyrkeby, gentleman of Stanbridge, John Marks, gentleman of Romsey, and a man from Wiltshire. They owed a debt of 40 marks (£13 13s 4d) to Sir William Capel, alderman of London, in respect of wool dealing. The Kyrkeby family were tenants of the manor of Stanbridge Earls for at least 250 years.

The largest profits, and probably the greatest risks, were thus made by those entrepreneurs who financed the cloths after production and before sale, and who were responsible for paying the ulnage.

Romsey Payers of the Ulnage
20 July 1394 - 22 November 1395

Name	Number of 'Dozens'	Tax	
		s	d
William Aleway	3		6¾
John Basset	4		9
Thomas Brangwayne	40	7	6
John Brewer of Romsey	32	6	0
Roger Byle	2		4½
John Clera Touker	8	1	6
John Coke	4		9
Peter le French Robert Touker William Touker Thomas Brangwayne	96 pieces of small cloths containing 33 pieces of cloth of assise	12	4½
Peter French of Romsey	46	8	7½
Peter le French	5		11½
Ralph Gervayse	6	1	1½
Gilbert Hosier	4		9
John Hulyn	2		4½
William Marchell	2		4½
John Mirghard	6	1	1½
Nicholas at Mount	4		9
Robert Palmer	3		6¾
John Penston	9	1	8¼
John Polayn	42	7	10½
John Pynchon	8	1	6
Richard Ryngston of Romsey	9	1	8¼
John Spaldyng	4		9
John Staunton	15	2	9¾
Robert Touker	3		6¾
William Touker	2		4½
William Touker jr	3		6¾
Robert Touker of Middlebridge	9	1	8¼
Robert Touker of Romsey	30	5	7½
William Touker of Romsey	36	6	9
John Wyght	13	2	5¼

Nevertheless, many fullers and dyers prospered, even though they were not the men making the greatest fortunes from this industry. Another group that made a substantial profit dealt in dyestuffs and other chemicals needed in cloth production.

The most affluent of these supply traders in the second quarter of the 15th century seems to have been Simon Long, one of Romsey's leading inhabitants between 1428 and 1451. He was named in the ulnage records in 1436, when he was accused of selling cloth that had not paid ulnage, although it is possible that he was pardoned and his cloth returned to him. His offence concerned 7 ells of black cloth valued at 10d an ell or 5s 10d altogether.

Simon Long's brush with the tax collectors does not seem to have done him any harm. In 1436, he was living in style in Church Street, a wealthy part of Romsey. By 1445, he also had a house with land around it in Southampton to the north of the Bargate. It was useful for him to have a base in Southampton, as he had an extensive trading operation there. The Southampton records show him sending madder, woad, weld, alum, oil, soap, wine and white and red herrings to Romsey around 1440. Madder, woad and weld are dyestuffs producing red, blue and yellow colours respectively. Alum is a mordant which affects how the dyes are accepted by the cloth. Oil and soap are used to process the cloth in the fulling and dyeing processes. The large quantities involved imply that Simon Long was acting as a wholesaler. Similarly, although some of the wine and herrings may have been for his own household, he probably sold some of them to fellow citizens.

Simon Long was not the only person caught trying to defraud the ulnage in Romsey. In 1444, a piece of red cloth, valued at £1 6s 8d, was seized from John Blake. A 'piece' was a whole cloth, 26 yards long. Nearly twenty years later in 1463, John Hosier was caught selling 15 yards of kersey worth 4d an ell or 5s 0d in all. Kerseys were narrower cloths than cloths of assise, and the ulnage he was trying to evade would have been minimal.

Other Romsey men were dealing in dyestuffs and further supplies for fullers and dyers. One of these was John Bocher, who was active in the 1440s, and dealt in a range of goods. In 1448, Bocher bought and transported several thousand slates for the roof of his own house. The location of his house is unknown, but this is another instance of the use of slates by wealthy Romsey townsmen. On a more regular basis, John Bocher received fulling and dyeing supplies from Southampton, some of which he sent to Salisbury.

Another with trading links with Salisbury was Nicholas Bryghtwyn, a fuller, who sent a consignment of teasels from Southampton to Salisbury in 1449. In September of that year, he had nearly a cart load of locks, a low quality wool, sent to him from Southampton. This wool would not have been used to make the high quality cloth that was processed under the auspices of the Italian merchants, but might have been intended for felt or stuffing.

Much of Romsey's industrial cloth-finishing was conducted under contract to the Italian merchants in Southampton. These men bought high quality English woollen cloth and exported it to Italy. Their willingness to have their cloth 'finished' in Romsey is a tribute to the standard of workmanship to be found in the town. However, the relationship was not without its problems. In 1450, men of Romsey marched to Southampton in order to protest about the prices the Italians were paying them for their work. The city fathers of Southampton, some of whom were Italian, were unsympathetic and set a watch for the rioters. When they reached the town, the authorities called out the militia and had the marchers imprisoned in Winchester gaol.

That the fullers and dyers of Romsey seem to have made comfortable livings can be seen by the fact that a number of them were appointed to office in the town, a role only available to the affluent. In 1467, John Baker, a fuller, was serving as the town's prepositus or manorial reeve. Another local man who was dealing in cloth and who became 'prepositus' in 1469 was William at Well. Two years earlier, the records show him paying ulnage on six cloths. The status reflected in this sort of financial venture is again consistent with evidence from Winchester, where people dealing in cloths were likely to hold civic office at some time or another.

The 1460s seem to have been a very good time for the Romsey cloth industry. The equivalent of 420 cloths of assise were charged with ulnage in 1467 - almost double that of 1394-5 - but interestingly only 18 people were involved, compared with 27 at the earlier date. This suggests that wealth was becoming more concentrated in the town.

The ulnage records continue to show men dealing in cloths who appear from all the other evidence to have no involvement with the cloth trade. In 1467, Richard Walkeleyn paid ulnage on 22 cloths. He was therefore a man of substance, for each cloth of assise had a minimum wholesale value of 13s 4d. He described himself as a butcher, although he was clearly active in a range of commercial ventures. He lived in Church Street in the house that had belonged to the affluent Simon Long a few decades earlier. He had another tenement near the Abbess's kitchen and her garden called 'Salve'. In 1467 Richard Walkeleyn acquired land in Ridge field, above Pauncefoot Hill. A widow, Juliana Levenoth, sold him all her lands, tenements, pastures, woods and rents in Ridge field which must have constituted a substantial holding. Richard died in 1471 and his widow, Alice, was later trading in property in her own right.

Other Enterprises
Although not in the same commercial league as the cloth-finishing industry, tanning continued to play an important part in the town's economic success. Many of the skins tanned and used to make leather goods were supplied by local butchers, but some were sent from Southampton, perhaps indicating a rise in production levels. Quality appears to have been high. In 1444 a Romsey tanner, Richard Noble, bought ten hides of fine white calf leather.

The business links with Southampton were strengthened throughout the 15th century, and involved a wide range of goods passing through the Southampton Bargate, and being recorded there in the town's brokage books. One Romsey entrepreneur was John Hosier who was involved in trading a wide range of commodities. In 1439, he received a quantity of wine in Romsey and 2000 slates; these are likely to have come from Devon. In 1443, his Southampton purchases included wax, wine, iron, and salt. He bought only four hundredweight of iron. This might have been required for traditional ironworking purposes, but the small amount involved may have been intended as a mordant in the dyeing process. Similarly, the salt could have been for either culinary or clothworking uses. On balance, the goods brought to Romsey by Hosier suggests that he was not himself a clothworker but more likely to have been an innkeeper who dabbled in investment opportunities. This conclusion is supported by the consignments that he received in 1448, which comprised wine, dried fruit and salt.

That Romsey men were trading in Winchester and Southampton can be seen from records in those cities' archives. In 1393, four men, William Wadman, Roger Faucon, Walter Burnham and Robert Barbour, were accused of selling wines at excessive prices in Winchester. In 1486, a Romsey cordwainer [shoemaker] named John William was fined for selling goods in Southampton without meeting the town's conditions for trading by outsiders.

Some of the neighbourhood's well-to-do and well-connected inhabitants supplemented their incomes by acting as royal tax-gatherers. In 1416, John Chamberlain 'of Romsey' became a Collector of the Tenths and Fifteenths in Hampshire. In 1453, one of the Collectors was William Smith of Wells by Romsey, who was also known as William Stonderoute, and, in 1468, William Moryng of Romsey was one of eight Collectors in the County, as was Edward Aillerigge in 1489. In the same year the same John Hamond who had lost the manor of South Wells to the Duke of Gloucester became Approver of the Ulnage, the official responsible for collecting the tax on high quality woven cloth. Interestingly, one of his guarantors, called a mainpernor, was Henry Burgeys of South Wells.

Urban Romsey in the Late 14th Century
There is no evidence about the size of Romsey's population before and after the Black Death, but, by the late 14th century, there was pressure on space for the congregation in the parish church. This may imply an increase in population.

The Abbey precinct and the adjacent market space occupied the centre of the long 'island' formed between the Test and the Fishlake/Holbrook. Romsey was not really big enough for

60

specialist streets, except for the 'Shambles', the name for the butchers' quarter. The large market space had yet to fall victim to the major encroachment that intruded in later years, and could accommodate both a general trading section and dedicated franchises for the more popular commodities, such as shoes or cheeses.

The main streets lay south and north of the Abbey. Newton Lane, Mill Street (now Bell Street), Banning Street, the lost Eny Street and Middlebridge Street lay to the south, while Church Street, Portersbridge Street, Mill Lane and Cherville Street lay to the north. The Broad Bridge across the Holbrook stream at the eastern end of the market area still marked the edge of the urban area. The bridge led to an area known only as 'beyond Broad Bridge'; the street called the Hundred was yet to develop, although Spittle Street led out to the leper hospital. There was a satellite settlement in the Latimer Street and Love Lane area, perhaps most easily reached via Porters Bridge. Everywhere else was countryside.

Romsey Properties
Much of the land and property in the town was owned by the Abbess. Some owners of country estates rented property from her, such as Stephen de Baldet who held an estate at Rumbridge in Eling, but rented a Romsey house from the Abbess at 2s 0d rent per annum. Other local landowners had their own town houses. A number of properties in Romsey, some of them in Bell Street, belonged to the manor of Wade, but they cannot be located more precisely. The Pauncefoot family also had property within the town, as well as a tenement in Banning Street. At that time, Banning Street was the main thoroughfare from Romsey to Southampton, so this might have been a good-sized suburban house.

Quite apart from the property held by the country gentry, the townspeople themselves were purchasing their own houses and land within Romsey, and some of them had substantial holdings. For example, in 1335, Albreda, the wealthy widow of Nicholas Spencer, sold to Alexander de Solrigge and his wife:

>A house in Churchbridge Street [probably in or near modern Church Street]
>A house in Middlebridge Street

61

A shop in Shambles, and 6d rent

A garden with a house on it in Eny Street in the west part called la Boresheye

Another garden in the east part of the same street

A third one there next to the garden of William Corbins

A fourth garden in a garden called la Wodehey in Eny Street

Also 2s 5d and 1lb of cummin annual rent from a tenement which John le Tailor and Joan his wife hold in Newton Street

2s 0d rent from a house which William Wappe once held in "Chepingestrete" [unidentified]

9d rent from a house in Bannock Street [Banning Street]

Also 1 acre of meadow in Tapsham mead [Tapsham Mead is at the end of Mill Lane]

And a plot of meadow at le morhe [unidentified]

Much of the information relating to medieval Romsey comes from the archives of Winchester College, and relates to their Romsey landholdings. The result is that some areas are better recorded than others, depending where the College property lay. One of the frequently mentioned parts of Romsey is the now lost Eny Street, which might otherwise be completely shrouded in mystery.

These old documents shed light on individual people. For example, John Shotter, a baker, would otherwise be unknown. In 1357 he bought a house and grounds in Eny Street, and eleven years later bought another property in the same street. He still held property in that street in 1381, when he acted as a witness for a neighbour. He bought more land in Eny Street in 1385, and a further piece in 1386 when he was described as John Shotter, senior.

The Shotter name is frequently found in the list of witnesses to other people's deeds, a sign that the family was highly regarded. In 1413, John Shotter described as 'of Romsey' became a Collector of the Tenths and Fifteenths in Hampshire. The name 'John Shotter' was used by several generations, and it is impossible to tell which one did what. It is clear, however, that 'John Shotter' continued to buy land in the Eny Street area, in Newton Street and elsewhere. Perhaps this was the beginning of an accumulation of wealth that enabled a subsequent member of the family to occupy the prestigious Embley estate in later centuries.

Romsey Town

Investment in the town indicated a sound level of economic confidence. One of the most prestigious developments was the *Swan Inn* on the north-west corner of the Market Place. It was owned by Winchester College and amongst their surviving deeds is a 21-year lease granting the inn to Thomas Kokys in 1477. The annual rent was 58s 9d with an extra 15d for the garden. At that time the *Swan* was described as a tenement or lodging house, with a kitchen, cellar and garden; William Taylour was the neighbour on the east (currently occupied by the Abbey National). As well as the property, certain fixtures and fittings were provided for the incoming tenant:

> First: 2 great chests whereof one of them is carved and the other serves to put oats in.
>
> Item: 11 bedsteads of which 3 are in the high turret over the great chamber, 2 in the chief chamber, 2 in the white chamber, 2 in the Howell chamber and one in the parlour.
>
> Item: in the great chamber is a long board, a pair of trestles and a form.
>
> Item: in the hall is a long shelf board and a bench and a bar of iron in the chimney there.
>
> Item: in the parlour is another bench.
>
> Item: in the kitchen is a dressing board, a bar of iron to hang pots and an old coop.
>
> Item: in the cellar is a board and a pair of trestles.
>
> Item: 3 stables racked and their mangers.
>
> Item: the said Thomas hath delivered to him by the said John 11 doors locked with their keys.

It is interesting to see how many beds were in some of the rooms, and that each room had its own name. The provision for horses would have been as important as that for human travellers, so the great chest for oats, and the stables, were essential if the house was to attract customers. It was common for kitchens to be separate from dwelling houses, because of the risk of fire, so the kitchen may have been in an outhouse to the rear of the property.

At the other end of the Market Place the *White Horse* was built or rebuilt in the early Tudor period. It was an outstanding building, on a prime site, and was probably sponsored by someone or some body of considerable power and wealth. Despite its 18th-century facade, the *White Horse* remains essentially a timber-framed building. Its coffee lounge still has original Tudor decoration painted onto the walls.

The Winchester College documents shed light on part of the northern side of Portersbridge Street. In 1461, Elena Bakon and her husband John leased a house on condition that it was

re-built with three high roofs. This house was between one belonging to the Abbey and a garden reached through 'a great gate' that lay next to Porters Bridge itself. In 1491, thirty years later, a building had been newly built and it was let to one William Molens. The houses on this site have recently been converted from solicitors' offices into private dwellings. The oldest is a timber-framed building and may be one of those referred to in these documents.

Portersbridge Street
where Elena and John Bakon agreed to
build a new house in 1461

The Town's Sense of Independent Security

Although the town continued to be governed by the Abbey, its new-found wealth gave it a greater independence. Its earlier successes had been under the protection of the Abbey, first as a source of work and then as an authority whose powers and privileges benefited the local inhabitants. Now there was a degree of autonomy amongst the business community. External factors, such as the London and Italian cloth dealers, had a major influence on the state of Romsey's economy. As the fortunes of the Abbey faded still further in the decades to come, the town was less affected than it would have been without these independent outside trade links.

Parish Church
The first known vicar of Romsey was Henry de Chilmark who was appointed in 1322. At that time the parish church was situated in the north aisle of the Abbey church. It was dedicated to St Laurence and was screened off from the rest of the building. The congregation could enter and leave by the north door without impinging on the nuns' use of the main part of the church. By 1372, this parish church within a church was in need of repair, and the Bishop of Winchester, William of Wykeham, ordered this to be put in hand.

By 1403 the north aisle was too small for the parish. The parishioners took their problem back to William of Wykeham. He endorsed their claim, declaring the north aisle to be inadequate for a town that was likely to become 'notable'. It was, he said, 'too little fitted for such a place, and for so large a population'. He therefore granted a licence for extensions to be made. The north transept of the abbey church was incorporated into the parish church as its chancel. An additional aisle was built, on the north side of the existing nave aisle, and archways were cut through the wall where once there had been windows. Thus the parish church was doubled in width and substantially lengthened. Later, the parish also acquired its own free standing bell tower, or campanile, and this stood in present-day Church Road, at the southern end of the terrace of houses.

Civic Authority
As the 14th century drew to a close, Romsey continued to accept the authority of the Abbess, despite its growing economic independence. There is no evidence that Romsey ever rebelled against the Abbey, even in the early 1300s when there were riots against a number of monasteries throughout the country. Nor is there any hint that the inhabitants sought to escape the lordship of the Abbess by purchasing borough status, as happened in some other towns. Maybe they were satisfied by the appointment of one of their prominent men as prepositus, or reeve, in which capacity he managed the town on behalf of the Abbess.

It seems likely that this office was only held for a year at a time, presumably out of necessity since it was unpaid. Contemporary records, including property deeds, show different men as prepositus, in a way that suggests frequent changes of office holder. For example, Thomas Brangwayn, who frequently acted as a witness to deeds, was described as 'prepositus' in 1390, but in 1394, he had no such title.

There were other public offices that needed men to undertake them. Thomas Bluet, who lived first in Latimer Street and then in Church Street, was required to serve on a Coroner's Jury in the 1390s. It is also possible that he was either prepositus or some other manorial official from time to time as people sought him out to witness their deeds.

One group that began to flourish in the late-14th century, as elsewhere in England, was that of lawyers. Their presence was a sign that the community was thriving. Amongst their number was John Foster or Forster, who was active in the property market on his own account as well as representing other people. His work probably included sorting out the affairs of families who had perished during the time of the Black Death.

In 1351, John Foster was the owner of part of the building on the north-west corner of the Market Place [later the *Swan Inn* and now the Conservative Working Men's Club]. In 1351 he bought a shop with a room over it in the Shambles. During his lifetime he bought various other properties, including the remaining portion of his Market Place tenement. When he was involved in property deals between other people, property was vested in him for legal purposes, so he was clearly a man of status and trust.

Romsey Extra
Much of eastern Romsey was in the hands of the Abbess, and known as her manor of Romsey Extra. For this estate the Abbess was answerable for taxation and other matters of royal administration first to the Hundred of King's Somborne and thence to the Sheriff of Hampshire. (Hundreds were the administrative sub-divisions of the county, a system from which the inner part of Romsey was exempt, as the Abbess answered directly to the sheriff.)

Somewhat confusingly, the name Romsey Extra was applied both to the entire rural manor, and also to one of the subdivisions, known as a tything. The tything of Romsey Extra was essentially the urban growth east of the Holbrook. The more rural tythings that evolved over time were Woobury (later Woodley), Lee, Wells, and Cupernham. Each tything was represented at the manor court, and its affairs separately recorded.

The Manor Courts
Several of the Manor Court Rolls for Romsey Extra survive from the 15th century. These records were mostly concerned with the transfer of manorial properties and local community matters. Tenants of the Abbess were fined for failing to repair their houses, and threatened with larger fines if the neglect continued. It is a little difficult to understand the level of fines; perhaps the sums set related to the individual's capacity to pay. Thus, in 1436, William Smyth of Lee was fined only 2d even though he had neglected his tenements so much that they perished. This was despite the fact that the Abbess had given oak worth 40d to help with repairs. Six years later, John Bassett of Love Lane was threatened with a much more daunting fine of 20s 0d if he did not complete his new house. Apparently, the framework was finished but he had failed to roof it in or enclose the walls.

Occasionally, these records also tell of individual bond tenants breaking free from manorial constraints - either by paying the lord of the manor for the privilege or by simply leaving without permission. The Streeche family illustrate this. John, son of Peter Streeche, had left in 1428. In 1436, his brother, Thomas, left the manor while another member of the family, Walter Streeche, was serving as bailiff. Walter's brother went off to be a soldier in 1444. By contrast, John Withergee of Lee paid 6d a year to live outside the manor.

Law and Order
Suspicious deaths might be the result of criminal action or merely domestic tragedy. In 1388, the Coroner was required to hold an inquest on Joan, the wife of William Bourelle. She had been found dead in her home in Romsey Extra with her neck broken. The explanation of her death was that she 'went up a

ladder towards her bed and she was very drunk and by misfortune she stumbled and fell to the ground'. The Coroner was assisted by a jury of 12 men of good standing, as well as representatives from Romsey Infra and the surrounding rural estates of Mainstone, Stanbridge and Wells.

Crime in the 15th Century

The Abbess also struggled with troublemakers in her manor. The neglectful William Smyth came before her courts on other matters. In 1436, he caused William Bretere's meadows to be flooded and damaged; a year later he was fined 6d for assaulting and insulting the bailiff, Walter Streeche. Poaching, a perennial problem in rural areas, was also rife. In 1435, John Sexsteyn and Thomas Talear dammed the watercourse by Street Mead, and took fish. In the following year, Thomas Welynow was caught taking hares from the Abbess's warren.

The New Forest was ever a temptation for poachers, some of whom operated on a commercial scale. Towards the end of the century, in 1486, John Calcayne, 'a yeoman recently of Romsey', hunted deer with greyhounds and killed a doe and young hind illegally. In the following year, William Dalle and Nicholas Pegeon, both butchers of Romsey, took a deer, with the aid of greyhounds. Pegeon was clearly not too particular about moral matters. In 1485, he had been fined 8d because his servant had stolen a candlestick in Southampton.

The Guild or Brotherhood of St George

Others were more spiritually inspired. The prosperity that came with industrial success probably encouraged the establishment of religious guilds or brotherhoods in Romsey. These were part of a popular trend among the affluent inhabitants of many towns, and enabled people to join together to establish chantries and employ priests to say masses for their souls and those of their families. Only the wealthiest people could afford to endow private chantries, but guilds opened up the opportunities for many more people to make communal provision.

The guilds served a wide social and religious purpose. In some ways they were forerunners of mutual aid societies, but with strong emphasis on spiritual as well as practical aims. Apart from the spiritual provision that was their primary motivation, they often arranged support for the families of members who had died.

The Tudor Rose
possibly built in the 15th century for the Guild of St George

There are hints of the existence of several religious guilds in Romsey. Those of St Christopher, of Our Lady and of Jesus have left a trace, mainly through mentions in wills, but the Brotherhood of St George was the most prominent. This guild was established before 1464 when Thomas Shotter bequeathed it 20s 0d in cash. A chantry came later, presumably when sufficient funds had accrued, and was founded on 17th February 1475 by letters patent of Edward IV.

The sense of unity evoked by membership of this guild was another manifestation of the growing individuality of the town. For the rest of its existence, the Brotherhood featured strongly in its members' wills. Many followed Thomas Shotter's example and bequeathed money or property to the guild.

Again, this was to the Abbey's disadvantage in terms of both authority and finance. The Abbess seems to have made no complaint, so must have resigned herself to the situation.

Thomas Leycroft died in 1530. He left 13s 4d to the Brotherhood of St George and 4d to the Brotherhood of Jesus. In his will he left much more money to religious observance than was customary. He left bequests, larger than usual, of 12d to Winchester Cathedral and 20d to the church of St Laurence in Romsey. He also left 6s 8d towards the church works of St Laurence's, 4d for the Trinity light, and 2d apiece for St Anthony's light, St Clement's light, St Rasym's light, St Katharine's light, St Blac's light, and St John's light. This list is interesting because it is probably a comprehensive record of the many lights, and hence altars, in the Abbey church of 1530 - just before the upheavals of the suppression. It also makes the only contemporary reference to the Saxon rood, the 'good rood in the Abbey's side' that is now on the exterior of the south transept, and to which Thomas assigned 4d. Thirteen years after his death, the name Leycroft was not in either the list of Abbey tenants or the tax return of 1543; so presumably the family had left Romsey by then.

An Abbess Disgraced: Elizabeth Broke
The Abbey was soon struggling with its own internal problems. Elizabeth Broke was elected as Abbess in 1472, and her behaviour thereafter caused much trouble for her community. Investigations made six years later led to her resignation. Strangely, after some complicated preliminaries, the sisters re-elected her, a move that suggests she had some qualities of leadership, however inappropriate they may have been to her calling. The nuns' choice was accepted by the Bishop, though he withheld the pastoral staff of authority for seven years.

In fact, the staff does not seem to have been restored to Elizabeth Broke until 1491, some 12 or 13 years later. In the following year, a report of a bishop's visitation makes more unhappy reading. This time the Abbess confessed to a debt of £80, and was held responsible for the appointment of a very unsatisfactory Steward by the name of Terbock. His spell in office had led to serious financial mismanagement. There were, moreover, implications of lax discipline resulting in nuns

70

going out into the town and frequenting local taverns. Many other complaints, petty or otherwise, conjure up a picture of a demoralised community that had lost its spiritual direction.

The Tudors and the Abbey

The arrival of the Tudors generally heralded a period of comparative peace in the town of Romsey, as it did for much of England, but for the monastic institutions of the country it was eventually to bring catastrophe.

The beginning of the 16th century did not mark a revival in the Abbey's fortunes. Indeed, a bishop's visitation of 27th March 1501 brought fresh accusations against the Abbess Elizabeth Broke. According to the evidence of the sisters, she failed to correct them but at the same time was cruel to them. Scandal was now rumoured about the Abbess and the infirmary chaplain, Master Bryce, who was said to have undue influence over her. Abbey properties within both the precinct and the town were badly neglected, and finances generally still poorly managed. It was probably a relief to the diocese when Elizabeth died in the following year, but the effects of her 30-year long abbacy made it difficult to restore the Abbey's tarnished reputation.

Unfortunately, Elizabeth Broke was succeeded by another unsuitable individual. Joyce Rowse was a greedy and lax leader who was quite the wrong person to restore the community to an even keel. Romsey Abbey was not the only English nunnery in disarray. In 1517, Bishop Fox issued an English version of the Rule of St Benedict in an attempt to provide nuns with a copy of the rule that they could understand since their education no longer included a working knowledge of Latin.

Anne Westbroke and Elizabeth Ryprose, the last two abbesses, seem to have been more worthy of their office, but by then the whole monastic system was under royal review. Abbess Ryprose tried hard to improve the state of affairs at Romsey. With the co-operation of her Steward, John Foster, she arranged for the rebuilding of the Abbey church tower and the chancel roof. The bells were re-hung just two years before the end came - all to no avail.

The Tudor Town

Henry VII came to the throne in 1485, but the Tudors belonged essentially to the 16th century. There is no evidence of any anti-Tudor elements in Romsey, so perhaps the two men who received royal pardons at the beginning of Henry VIII's reign were guilty only of some taxation offence. John Ray, merchant, and Robert Reynold, glover, do not sound like common criminals, and members of their families certainly became solid successful citizens in later centuries. A more obvious offence had been committed by William Carpenter, a Romsey smith, who, in 1537, received a pardon for a theft at Bramshaw. With two other men he had broken into the church and stolen a silver gilt cup, an altar cloth and other articles belonging to the parishioners. Although the thieves were pardoned, it is not recorded whether the Bramshaw parishioners ever saw their treasures back. Usually, offenders were accused of more prosaic crimes, such as that of William Baker of Romsey, fined in 1513 for selling bread that was short measure.

A Tudor property in Palmerston Street

Romsey suffered from epidemics in the early part of the century. A rare royal visit was cancelled by Henry VIII in 1526 for fear of 'the sickness', and, as in other places, plague and lesser scourges continued to visit the town from time to time.

Nevertheless, Romsey people were becoming increasingly confident under the leadership of the prepositus, or reeve, who may have been acting more and more independently in response to the inadequate guidance of the Abbess or her Steward. The term 'mayor' was favoured, first rather tentatively by John Pecy in 1507, who was described as 'mayor or prepositus', and then more decisively by William Scragge two years later. Such terminology does not, however, mean that the town was a borough at this stage.

Economically, the town was probably not as buoyant as it had been in the 15th century. There was a general decline in the cloth trade through Southampton as the Italian merchants withdrew, and this must have affected Romsey. Romsey seems to have responded by widening the sphere of its cloth work as 16th-century wills reveal that sheep were being reared locally, a practice for which there is no earlier evidence. There was more weaving than previously. Fulling continued, as shown when John Blowes left his fuller's shears to his kinsmen. Dyeing also continued, and dyeworks were located by the waterways of Church Street and Portersbridge Street.

It was probably a time of mixed fortunes. Richard Goldering, who died in 1529, seems to have been overtaken by catastrophe. Part of his will reads:
> The residue of my goods I would my wife should have to dispose for my soul's health, but as God knows, my debts be so sore that I fear she shall enjoy no part of it. Therefore I pray that John Reynolds and my ghostly father for to see my poor body buried.

By comparison Robert Dixon, who died in 1545, left an intact fortune that included a dozen or so silver spoons, six of which were ornamented with lions. The main ultimate beneficiary of his house and most of his goods was his son, Richard, but each of his men-servants was to receive 8d and each maid-servant 4d. The whole tenor of the will suggests a comfortable life.

The Dissolution

King Henry VIII's matrimonial difficulties became the focus of his dispute with the Pope and led to the secession of the English church from the church of Rome. As part of the re-organisation, Henry began to dissolve monasteries and similar institutions, and to confiscate their property.

Despite its many problems, Romsey Abbey was still sufficiently substantial to escape the first wave of closures. The warning signals of the first suppressions initiated a flurry of self-interest among Abbey employees and an unseemly scramble for Abbey assets. Sir Richard Lyster of Stanbridge wrote to Thomas Cromwell on 15th September 1538, advising that 'The Monastery of Romsey, hearing they are in danger of suppression, are making leases and alienating their goods'. He desired to know 'whether he should stay them in this'.

Sir Richard was not simply a busybody neighbour but held high office under the crown as Chief Baron of the Exchequer in 1530 and Lord Chief Justice of Common Pleas in 1546, by which time he had moved to Southampton. His concern does not appear to have aroused much response.

In December 1538, John Foster, the last Abbey Steward, wrote a very long letter to Sir Thomas Seymour, brother of Henry VIII's third queen, Jane Seymour. He gave a brief description of the monastic house and the names of the nuns, together with a breakdown of the Abbey estates. It is not apparent from the letter whether it was written with the agreement of the Abbess, or whether he was pursuing his own interests.

Closure eventually came in 1539. Romsey was possibly deemed to have obstructed the royal will, for it seems that no financial provision was made for the nuns, as was the case in many monasteries. The 25 nuns were dispersed; with only one exception they vanish from the records.

John Foster was the only person to emerge with long-term benefits, and he may have been protected by his influential patron, Sir Thomas Seymour. The link with the Seymours was strengthened by his marriage to a member of the family, Jane Wadham. She had been one of the nuns, but at the investigation that followed their marriage she argued that she had not taken her vows voluntarily. This was accepted, and their marriage was recognised as legal.

As early as 1536, John Foster had arranged a pension for himself relating to the chapels of St Andrew and St Peter. This amounted to £20 6s 8d annually, and was continued after the Dissolution for the rest of his life. With other property income, John and Jane Foster moved to North Baddesley, south of

Romsey, to live in a house that had belonged to the Knights Hospitaller.

The Crown continued to honour the obligations of monastic institutions just for the life-time of those in receipt of any charities at the time of the Dissolution. Thus, in 1539, the beneficiaries of the two charities established under King Edgar's 10th-century charter were protected. The Poor Sisters living in a house called 'the Sisters' House' by the Abbey gateway had been accustomed to an annual allowance of 40s 0d each, but this was halved after the Dissolution. The Spittle, or Hospital of St Mary Magdalene and St Anthony, which provided shelter for both men and women, was caring for ten men and women in 1539. When the Spittle House was finally sold by the king in 1544, the only tenant was Henry Warner. It is not clear whether he was warden for any remaining paupers or whether he was himself the sole survivor of the one-time inmates.

The buildings of most monastic institutions were destroyed so that they could not be re-inhabited and used by their former occupants. There are stories of roofs being removed, and their timbers used as firewood, as the lead from the roof and gold and silver wares were melted down to be sent to London as bars of metal. Only items of the very finest workmanship were preserved. Henry VIII's coffers benefited enormously, but England lost much of its fine Saxon and medieval heritage.

In Romsey, the Abbey church posed a problem. Since part of it had served as the parish church, Romsey would have been left without a place of worship if it had shared the fate of similar buildings. The King may have been removing the English church from Papal domination, but he had no intention of doing away with religion in England. Therefore, the church of Romsey Abbey was allowed to keep its roof, and five years later the building was sold to the town for £100. Somehow the town rallied round to find this money, a huge sum for the day. The royal deed of sale, still displayed in Romsey Abbey, granted to the townsfolk the church, a narrow processional way around it and land for a cemetery. No other Abbey lands or income were included, and the town has had to support the church ever since. Fairly soon after the purchase, some alterations were made to the building. The additional north aisle was removed, and the Lady Chapel behind the high altar was demolished.

Since the town had no formal local government, it was necessary to recognise the churchwardens as a body corporate to act as the purchaser. The four churchwardens, whose names are enshrined in the deed of sale, were Robert Cook, John Salt, John Ham and John Knight.

There is no clear evidence to show how the town was governed between the closure of the Abbey in 1539 and the establishment of the town as a borough in 1607.

A tax roll from 1543 sub-divided Romsey with separate entries for the town and the districts of Cupernham, Extra, Cherville Street, Wobere, Lee, and Roke. Among the inhabitants listed are the four men who bought the Abbey church on behalf of the town. The charges against their names show them to have been amongst the wealthiest men in the town

    Robert Cook, 13s 4d
    John Salt, 14s 8d
    John Ham, 14s 8d
    John Knight (of Cupernham) 13s 4d

A few others could match them. Leaving aside the gentry, the following also paid 13s 4d:

    Walter Carter
    C. Segewyke
    Robert Bore of Wobere
    Thomasina Tyngell (the only high-paying woman)

Interestingly, in view of the decline in the Italian trade, several inhabitants had Italian names, such as Guido Bishop or Manristo Lyght. One person, Nicholas Cosset, was described on the list as an alien but this does not necessarily mean that he was non-English.

At some stage, worship was transferred to the main part of the church. It is noticeable that people went on referring to St Laurence as the dedication of their parish church for many years after the Dissolution of the monastery, even though the main church is dedicated to St Mary and St Ethelfleda. The chapel of St Laurence is still to be found in the north transept.

The rest of the Abbey's property and estates were taken into the hands of the crown, along with all the other monastic lands that King Henry had seized. Gradually, the lands in Romsey were sold to entrepreneurs who in turn sold them on to more permanent owners. The inhabitants of the town could only wait and see who their new landlords were to be.

In 1545, the monastic precinct was leased to Peter Westbroke for a period of 21 years at an annual rent of 26s 8d, with Westbroke responsible for the repairs. Some of the site was occupied by John Richardson as tenant. Richardson had not been on the tax roll of the year before, so either he was not wealthy, or

Temple Buildings, The Abbey
on part of the site of the
nuns' domestic range

he had moved into the area after that taxation list was compiled. In 1546, the year after the Westbroke lease, the precinct was sold to two property speculators from Yorkshire, John Bellow of Grimsby and Robert Biggott of Wharram, who seem to have had no other links with the town.

Their deed of sale included a description of the area, although not one that by itself can be used to reconstruct the Abbey complex. The property included a mansion called the Abbess's lodging, which abutted the chapel of St Peter. In addition there was a kitchen, a granary, a stable and a barn in the outer court of the Abbey. Along the boundary walls were premises including those occupied by John Richardson - the Gatehouse, a house called the Clerk's chambers and a chamber called the Receiver's lodging. Closer to the church were other buildings, including the dorter and frater, the nuns' sleeping and eating quarters. The lead from the roofs of these latter buildings was excluded from the sale, which suggests that it was stripped off and the buildings made uninhabitable.

A few of the Abbey meadows were sold along with the monastic buildings. These were called Tapsham, Langley Mead, Goosemead, and South Garden. Although Bellow and Biggott bought all this property, they quickly sold on to Francis Fleming in December 1546. Some other Romsey land was also in short-lived ownership. Those estates that had been granted to Sir Thomas Seymour, in early favour as Edward VI's uncle, were taken back into royal hands when Seymour fell from grace.

The Effect on the Town

In 1544, the Abbey's main secular holding in Romsey was sold to John Foster and Richard Marden for £900 53s 7d. This sale included some lands in nearby Wellow as well as a substantial part of Romsey. The grant lists all the tenants, names many of the lands, and complements the tax return of the same year. Some of the tenants listed in the sale document were the descendants of those mentioned in the manorial court records at the beginning of the century. Richard Marden disappeared from the scene very early on. In 1549, Foster sold this Romsey estate to Francis Fleming, who had already acquired the Abbey precinct.

In 1545, John Foster, this time with Thomas Thoroughgood, bought a large parcel of lands from the Crown, including several mills in Romsey. Amongst the property acquired by Foster was the 13th-century stone building now called *King John's House.*

The land in Romsey Extra 'beyond Broad Bridge' started to become more clearly defined during the Tudor period. The name of 'The Hundred' first began to creep into general use during the early part of the 16th century. In the 1540s both Henry Levermore and John Alone were said to have houses and gardens that were overlooked by a house in the Hundred. Spittle Street remained in use in the 16th century. It seems to have lain to the north of the present line of The Hundred.

The walls round the Abbey precinct were removed although this did not give an open vista because the Abbey was surrounded by encroaching buildings. The one-time walls present a puzzle because archaeological evidence for them is very patchy, although the documents refer to them quite emphatically as stone walls, not just walls. They were probably made of flint, as there is little evidence of re-used stonework around the locality, as in some other ex-monastic towns.

Further Reforms
The ecclesiastical reforms that were put under way by Henry VIII were continued under the regime of his son, Edward VI. Not content with closing down all monasteries, the government closed all the chantries. In the case of Romsey, the Brotherhood of St George was abolished, along with any lesser brotherhoods. If the other brotherhoods had property it is not apparent from the records, but that of St George had acquired a useful portfolio of lands in and around Romsey. The confiscation of these properties seems somewhat unfair because they had been bought by the pious donations of local people, but questioning the actions of a Tudor monarch was not generally considered diplomatic. The St George's property was sold to William Wynlowe and Richard Felde of London, two property speculators. It was described thus:

> the house in tenure of Thomas Flecher in the street called Market Place in Romsey, Hants,
> a chamber within the churchyard there in tenure of William Michell, clerk,
> a house in tenure of Richard Carter in the street called Middlebridge Street in Romsey,
> another with a garden in that street in tenure of Robert Bull,
> a house called le Cocke and a garden in Cherville Street in tenure of Edward Loder,
> 3 houses and garden there in the several tenures of Emma Cornelys, widow, Louis Barret and John Richardes,
> and 2 houses in Church Street, Romsey, in tenure of William Purfysshe and Walter Gasshe.

The Town Survives
Despite the uncertainties of the cloth industry following the end of the great Italian trade, and the unsettling events of the Dissolution, mid-16th-century Romsey had its share of prosperous inhabitants. The continued, if changing, existence of the cloth industry is shown by the will of John Blowes, fuller, who died in 1549. Appraisers valued his estate at £64 5s 0d

which made him one of the richest men in Romsey. He left two houses in Middlebridge Street, and another house with an acre of land in Cherville Street. He gave his cousin Thomas, 'a little plot of ground on the west side of his house'. He also owned property in Stoneham, near Southampton. In 1544, he had been tenant of one of the Abbey's messuages in Middlebridge Street, paying 6s a year for it. This property belonged to the manor and therefore could not feature in his will.

John Blowes' goods and chattels were assessed for probate, and they give an indication of the extent of his business interests. Perhaps changing circumstances in the cloth trade had encouraged him to diversify, for in his warehouse he had 14 barrels of honey and 1½ cwt of wax. He also had vats and a honey press with honey bags, as well as weighing equipment. He was obviously dealing in honey and wax production as well as cloth-processing.

His workshop, however, also bore strong evidence of the continuing importance of his cloth interests. It contained apparatus for processing cloth after fulling, including six pairs of fuller's shears (to trim the nap) and a board on which to deal with the cloth, burling irons for extracting knots from cloth, and a press for treating the cloths. He also owned 1120 lbs of wool worth £40. The debts due to him included one of 5s 0d for dyeing wool owned by William Blowes. It seems likely that he did business in his hall where he had a counter and a carpet with a banker cloth - a chequered cloth on which calculations could be made much in the manner of an abacus.

John Blowes died just as the ancient Abbey-based structure of Romsey was passing away, and the town was about to enter a sixty years hiatus, for which little is known of its governance, although it continued to thrive. The Tudor period that had started well-rooted in its medieval past had evolved into a time of fundamental change.

Part II

1550
to
1900

Author/Co-ordinator
Barbara Burbridge

Photographic Work Charles Burnett

Contributors
Pat Genge, Nancy Kelly, Joy Knowles, Jessica Spinney

The north side of Romsey Abbey
showing changes that have happened to the nave aisle wall
since the medieval extension was pulled down
after the Dissolution of the Abbey

The two windows nearest the porch were originally set into the outer wall of the extension, and were re-used to block the archways that once linked the extension to the main north aisle. The two Romanesque windows to the left are Victorian replacements, while the north porch is even later, having been built with the proceeds of the 1907 Romsey Pageant.

1550-1603: ADJUSTING TO CHANGE

By 1550, the townspeople had had eleven years in which to come to terms with the departure of the nuns from Romsey Abbey. They had had just six years to grow accustomed to the overwhelming fact that the Abbey church was now, in its entirety, their parish church, where, by edict of 1538, their births, deaths and marriages were recorded in the parish register. Within that church they were presumably adapting to the first English Book of Common Prayer introduced in 1549 by Archbishop Cranmer. During the next decades there would be further food for thought in the ideas trickling through from the Continent, where the reforming theologies of Martin Luther and John Calvin were taking root. By the 1590s, the national law had placed an obligation on all those over 16 years of age to attend the Church of England. Bye-laws imposed restrictions on secular activities - particularly 'tippling' - during the times of divine service. Although the Abbey community had gone, its church remained at the heart of Romsey life.

The Old Monastic Precinct

The southern domestic area of the monastic precinct, sold off initially to the entrepreneurial pair, Bellow and Biggott, was now in the hands of the Fleming family of Broadlands. The Flemings may well have bought this property within the town in order to establish a manorial mill. As the Abbey's Town Mills and those at Mill Lane were either sold off by John Foster or passed to his son, Andrew, it is possible that the Flemings saw the

Site of first Abbey Mill
viewed from Abbey Water

potential of the Abbey Water site. This idea is supported by the fact that, so far, the mill on this site cannot be dated before the time of the Fleming ownership.

83

Some of the nearby existing buildings, such as the Abbey gateway and the Clerk's chambers, with the Receiver's lodging beyond, were then leased out by successive owners of Broadlands. As late as 1684, such a lease carried the proviso that the tenant should grind his corn at the Abbey Mill, thus endorsing its status as a manorial mill, and showing how some feudal elements persisted.

As all the various changes took place, many inhabitants must have been genuinely shocked, bewildered and cautious, still looking back to a system that had endured for over 600 years. Others must have been more directly worried about their own livelihoods, having depended on work within the monastic precinct. But there were some who welcomed the challenge, ambitious for themselves and for the town of Romsey.

The Population of Tudor Romsey

The word 'town' was once used more as an indication of a special function - a market or port, for example - than of size. Even though urban growth was a feature of the 16th century, it was only comparative, and few towns had more than 2,500 inhabitants. The community of Romsey in which such stirring events were happening was very small.

It was also a very young community. Life-expectancy was improving nationally in Tudor times but it was still in the low forties. Consequently, it is thought that rather more than a fifth of the total population was under ten - and that was in spite of the high rates of infant mortality.

It is very difficult to work out population figures for Tudor Romsey, but there can be little doubt that the town grew, albeit irregularly, during the 16th century. Some idea of Romsey's population may be deduced from various tax returns, such as the lay subsidy of 1586. Analysis suggests that Romsey Infra and Romsey Extra together then had around 1,200 inhabitants.

The first useful national survey was made right at the end of the Elizabethan era, in 1603, primarily as an investigation, instigated by Archbishop Whitgift, into the pattern of church-going within each parish. The local incumbent was requested to report the number of communicants of the Church of

England, the number of Papists and the number of non-communicants in his particular parish. The accuracy of the results must have varied greatly according to the enthusiasm and competence of the individual concerned. There is also uncertainty about just who was included in the survey, though it is assumed that all men and women over 16 years of age were counted, since they were all legally obliged to attend the official Protestant church. The handful of non-attenders recorded in Romsey for 1603 - just 30 non-communicants and 3 Papists - would have had to pay a fine for upholding their principles.

By using an agreed multiplier of 1.5, to account for the numerous children of the town, a rough population count emerges, but one that should be treated with due caution. It suggests that Romsey in 1603 was a fairly typical market town of its time with 1500-2000 people at most. This number implies a spurt in population size over the years following 1586. If correct, such a growth was probably due to migrants, drawn to town life, as much as to improved life-expectancy.

The town would have been considerably smaller during the greater part of the previous century. In such a small community, the merge between urban and rural activities was still almost unnoticeable. Many people, of necessity, had to pursue more than one occupation according to the season. Records reveal that tradesmen often had strips in the town fields while, conversely, agricultural workers turned to weaving and other crafts at quiet times in the farming calendar.

In support of the notion of a positive if uneven rise in population, the Romsey parish registers show that births generally outnumbered deaths in the final decades of the 16th century, indicating an overall growth. But there were some disastrous years when the reverse applied. Between 1569 and 1603 there were about a dozen years when deaths rose above births, although the difference was just ten or under in half of those years. Other years were more worrying, especially 1597. In that year there were 119 deaths against 42 births, making a daunting margin of 77 more deaths than births. Such depressing figures were often linked to poor harvests, resulting in famines that weakened people's resistance to disease.

To their great relief, however, the later Tudors were no longer threatened by the appallingly swift destruction of the 'sweating sickness' that had haunted their predecessors. This infection seems to have disappeared as mysteriously as it came, though many still continued to use the term for similar, but generally less lethal, complaints. In a comparatively peaceful era, and famine-pestilence apart, people's health improved, perhaps only marginally, but enough for England's population to increase.

Trade and Industry

Boosted by both incomers and a rising birth-rate, the economy of late Tudor Romsey was important to a large area around the urban centre. The weekly market itself was a commercial focus. It was mainly an agricultural market with a range of farm produce on offer - from livestock to cheeses and vegetables - but it also dealt in more personal items, such as clothing. Stallholders, itinerant pedlars and farmers' wives displayed their goods, cattle were bought and sold, local and national news exchanged. No doubt, there was also a smattering of gossip, for market day was probably a social event for many. *The White Horse* and *The Swan* offered hospitality on the north side of the Market Place. The permanent shops - workshops where goods were produced as well as sold - would be anxious to benefit from the custom brought in by the market.

Many people came to market from the rural surroundings. Some were affluent, like several generations of the Ray family at Cupernham. The Rays had a mixed farm of cattle and crops that included wheat, barley, oats and peas. John Kitchener, yeoman of Mainstone, owned a considerable amount of pewter and brassware - and a bible. Living just beyond, in a well-stocked farm on Pauncefoot Hill, John Denham's bed had a silk tester and silk hangings, and there were painted cloth hangings around the chamber. John Denham also had a small collection of books, and his title of 'gentleman' seems well-justified. These men, and others with smaller holdings, brought their cattle to the market, first stage in a chain that ran through rural and urban Romsey. From the farmers the cattle passed to the butcher who sent the hide to the tanner. After the basic leather had emerged from the smelly tanneries, it went to the leather 'dresser' and thence to the craftsmen who made boots and shoes, saddles and horse collars and other items of use or ornament.

Romsey Market Place, showing the historic *Swan Inn*
before 20th-century alterations were made

Inventories taken after a tradesman had died often included his working tools. The tanners had small bark mills for extracting tannin (mostly from oak-bark), together with vats, shovels, and skins. Clothworkers left fuller's shears, looms and burling irons. Carpenters bequeathed their edged tools, only the tips being finished in expensive metal. John Levermore, blacksmith, died in 1588 leaving two forges, an anvil, a hammer, bellows, tongs, pincers and a stock of iron. His death, at a time when he was still clearly active in his trade, must have caused difficulties for many who relied on his services.

A slightly different aspect of Romsey business is revealed in the possessions of a widower named Thomas Smarte. He was a barber who was assisted by his son while his daughters, Sysley and Millred, kept house for them all. The list of his working equipment, made when he died in 1594, betrays fleetingly the vanity of some of his customers. In his workshop he had two

87

chairs, two looking glasses, two brushes, 14 washing basins, three dozen towels and three cases of scissors and razors, together with small grinding stones to keep all sharp. There are signs also of his side-line as a local 'surgeon' - two cases of instruments and salves or ointments.

Romsey's fulling mills, timelessly pounding great lengths of woven cloth, shared the waterways with the corn mills. Early conflicts about water power may be traced to this period, and Andrew Foster, son of the last Abbey Steward and owner of Mead Mill, continued a dispute that had erupted in his father's time with the owner of Spursholt Mill (later Sadler's Mill).

Snippets of information suggest that working life in Romsey was hard in modern terms. The curfew bell was tolled at 5am and 8pm. At one time the morning curfew had sounded even earlier, at 4am, for the benefit of the clothiers when their industry was at its peak. The slight relaxation to the start of the day may reflect the downturn in Southampton's fortunes as London and Italian financial investment diminished. Despite this, however, dealing in woollen cloth continued to sustain Romsey's economy throughout the Tudor period and beyond. Many entrepreneurial clothiers built up substantial fortunes, and other tradesmen established good businesses as well.

John Suter, a mercer, died in 1591. At a time when very few Romsey people left estates exceeding £100 in value, his inventory shows him to have been worth £576 28d, though it has to be said that £411 4s 8d of this consisted of debts due to him. His house and contents were appraised for valuation soon after his death. This appraisal shows that his home had a hall, parlour, kitchen (off which was a boulting house where flour was sifted) and a shop. There were lofts over both the parlour and the shop, a cellar beneath the house and stables in the 'backside'. The shop was a treasure trove containing some 176 items, which conjure up a lively picture of the shop itself and the likely appearance of Mr Suter's customers around the town.

The stock varied from 7 yards of moth-eaten frise [a coarse woollen cloth] worth only a shilling to half a piece of straw-coloured William fustian [a coarse cotton and flax mix] at 45s 0d and lace braid at 40s 0d. Amongst a wide range of differing cloths,

John Suter sold red, blue and tawdry cotton; Holland and brown Holland [bleached and unbleached linen]; coarse northern canvas; black frise; striped, ash-coloured and straw-coloured sack-cloth; brown and sand-coloured fustian; black and crimson durance [a stout cloth]; striped or blue and white aproning; and flannel. Boot-hose fringe, crimson and black silk fringe, silk and coarse ribbons and braids and threads of different colours were all for sale. As side-lines, Mr Suter also offered such diverse items as bowstrings at 3d a dozen or ABC books and primers. The local inhabitants must have enjoyed going to examine the wide range of goods on offer.

Romsey Fashions

The names of John Suter's customers may be unknown, but there are others who were named in wills and wore the clothes bequeathed to them by friends and family. After Alice Cox died in 1556, Agnys Walys was probably delighted with the red kirtle she inherited, though she may have envied Isobel Hayward who became the new owner not only of a violet kirtle, but also Alice's second best petticoat, an apron and a kerchief. Such passed-on finery must have needed much alteration unless clothes were left to 'fit where they touched'.

Although it was generally the women will-makers who described their clothes in greatest detail, some men also thought carefully about bequeathing their clothes, matching garments to personalities. Thus Richard Freeborne left Father Saywell, the priest, a suitably decorous black sleeved jacket that reached to his knees, but bequeathed to Robert Wisdom a much more stylish outfit of a fine white doublet, a russet jerkin and breeches.

The Market Place was where the best-dressed people might be seen. There walked Nicholas Sedgewick in a velvet gown trimmed with feshan [the fur of the polecat] and John Barnard in a violet gown. They may have bowed politely to Esabell Wellys in her tawny gown trimmed with otter fur, or another one she had, lined with satin of Cyprus and trimmed with black velvet. She in turn may have felt upstaged by Alice Duke, peacocking in a gown embroidered with gold or Agnes Sedgewick in her gown edged with white fur over a worsted kirtle trimmed with tawny velvet.

The bright colours of these expensive clothes that only the more affluent townsfolk could afford must have blazed out in contrast to the dull coarse clothes in fairly dingy shades of brown that proclaimed the poor labouring family. Clothes, indeed, cost such a high percentage of earnings that even the better-off people were grateful for the gowns and doublets that came their way in the wills of fellow citizens.

Growing Up in Tudor Romsey

Most of the many youngsters of Romsey, dressed in similar style, were learning the family way of life from very early years - farmworkers' children scaring the birds or picking stones out of the way of the plough, the town children sweeping the workshop floor or fetching and carrying for a range of craftsmen. Only a very few boys received any formal education, and the girls generally learned domestic skills at their mothers' side. The son of Richard Freeborne of Whitenap was one of the fortunate ones. When Richard died in 1591 he desired 'Elin my wife shall give unto my Son meat and drink and lodging and all manner of apparel whatsoever and to keep him at School and to bring him up in learning'. Little is known, however, of any school where Richard's son might have been educated.

Something of the expected relationships between the generations comes to life in the will of George Barton, a woollen draper. This will, dated 1589, included the following:

> 'My will is that my wife shall be with my son Peter Barton and he to keep her and allow her all necessaries which belongeth for a mother. And he to use her honorable and Reverently with soberness and equitie as a child ought to use his mother'.

This same George Barton also left 'towards the reparation of Middlebridge five shillings'. Middlebridge, then a three-arched stone bridge, was in a perilous state for decades but would not be replaced until the 1780s; it was not the only bridge with a problem.

The Tudor Townscape

The network of waterways in and around Romsey meant that there were countless bridges of varying size and importance throughout the town. Most of them seem to have been largely made of timber, and the consequent rotting led to a constant need for repairs, a situation that persisted for centuries.

The actual lay-out of Tudor streets was unchanging within Romsey Infra, but 'beyond Broad Bridge' the street newly called The Hundred was replacing Banning Street as the way to Southampton (see map on page 100). It is thought that the medieval route south via Banning Street fell into disfavour during the post-Dissolution years, when the new residents at Broadlands probably did not welcome the closeness of the busy road to their home. An alternative way was identified, and the road beyond the east end of the Market Place was diverted slightly southwards to cut a new route, via a natural low contour, towards and along present-day Palmerston Street. The Southampton road, as it was called until the 19th century, then continued due south along a line now within Broadlands Park. This new way south was considered, at the time, to be satisfactorily distant from the Flemings' house.

Within the town, the street fronts were gradually filling up. Between the dwellings and workshops were narrow walk-through entries and the occasional wider openings for carts, all leading to a jumble of outbuildings in the 'backsides'.

A surprising number of Romsey's present houses date from the 16th and 17th centuries. An increased use of flint or brick foundations lifted timbers above the damp earth and thus enabled buildings to survive. Many, though, were later given smart brick facades that still hide the timber-framing within. Only uneven ridges and generally low elevations betray the true age of these properties from the outside.

In an area devoid of local stone, the available materials dictated that ordinary buildings were predominantly timber-framed. Houses along the central streets were often tiled, but outbuildings and lesser properties were all thatched, as were many of those distant from the town centre. The *Old Thatched Cottage* in Mill Lane and the thatched cottages at the lower end of Middlebridge Street illustrate the more commonly found building style in Tudor Romsey, but even so these were probably larger than average, and occupied by better-off inhabitants.

King John's House, built of stone and flint, continued as an exception outside the old monastic precinct. Already 300 years old, it was transformed into a domestic building after Henry VIII had disposed of it as one of his acquisitions following the dissolution of Romsey Abbey. Within time, the old stone house acquired a Tudor fireplace and a timber-framed partition to the lower floor. The easterly section of this lower part became a workshop for a succession of craftsmen. A typical timber-framed extension followed, probably in the next century (despite bearing the name of *Tudor Cottage*).

Tudor Cottage
with King John's House in the background

Inside a Tudor Home

The quality of life inside these homes improved during the Tudor period. William Harrison, writing about English homes in 1587, noticed 'the multitude of chimneys lately erected'. Before then, smoke from fires had generally escaped through louvres in the roof. He reported improvement in sleeping comforts or, as he phrased it, an 'amendment of lodging'. People had 'lain full oft upon straw pallets, on rough mats covered only with a sheet, under coverlets made of dagswain or hopharlots and a good round log under their heads instead of a pillow'. Further signs of affluence were seen in tableware where wooden platters had been increasingly abandoned in favour of pewter; wooden spoons for silver or tin.

Not everyone shared this improved style of living. When John Bayliye died in Romsey, in 1571, his inventory consisted only of two cattle worth 40s 0d and ready money totalling 18s 0d - hardly an excess of luxury. John Bayliye was just one Tudor person whose life-styles are discovered in their wills and inventories. Other inhabitants were obviously benefiting from the improvements recorded nationally by William Harrison.

Their wills often reveal several aspects of their lives, besides describing the clothes or tools that they handed on.

Tudor Wills

The more spiritual ethos of the day is discernible in the preambles of wills. These dealt with the important concerns of body and soul before the bequests to family and friends and the appointment of executors and overseers. The wording is sometimes a reminder of the religious see-saw that dogged the middle of the 16th century. If Mary Tudor had lived long enough to fulfil her dream of restoring the old Catholic faith, then the tone of Alice Cox's 1556 will might have been more commonplace. As well as committing her soul to Almighty God, Alice desired, with traditional fervour, 'Our Lady St Mary and all the Company of Heaven to pray for me'.

Regardless of the religious mood of the moment, the Tudor will-maker was consistently anxious about the disposal of his body and the future of his soul. To that end his conscience often needed to be soothed by the making of charitable gifts. Although small sums of money to the parish church of St Laurence and the mother church of St Swithun in Winchester were long deemed sufficient, some wished to do more. Late Tudor wills reflect the changing religious background to these 'preamble' bequests. No longer did they feature donations to the Guild of St George in Romsey, now dissolved.

Chantries having been banned, the more affluent left sums of money to be handed out to the poor at the funeral and later anniversaries. In this way, the dying still hoped to be remembered and have prayers said for them. It was a worthy change of direction. With the departure of the nuns, there was a void in local support of the poor, so the vogue for leaving money directly to those in want was mutually beneficial. The 'poor man's box' improved the lot of the needy and assuaged consciences; with luck, it bought a few prayers for the departing soul.

A rather more practical form of charitable bequest also became a popular item in the preamble of a will. In 1553, Nicholas Carpynter left a few pence for church repairs; perhaps the Abbey church extension had already been pulled down making

93

it necessary to re-instate the north aisle walls. In 1558, John Kirkeby of Stanbridge Earls left 12d to the parish church to be spent on the 'paving healing and appointing of the covering of the north aisle', in which he wished to be buried 'a little above the pew belonging to the house of Stanbridge Earls.

There were other ways in which the dying tried to assist the community. In 1571 Simon Clarke left 13s 4d 'for the hanging of the bells in the tower'. This money must have been held in trust for some time; the re-hanging of the parish bells in the tower and the pulling down of the old parish belfry were not properly sorted out until the next century.

After the preamble came the main thrust of the will, the disposal of the testator's worldly goods. The 1571 will of Alexander Gasse, butcher, contains a minefield of family bequests with plenty of opportunity for argument about which pot or pan might be considered to be the best, finest, thinnest or whatever the description might try to convey - a hazard that permeates countless similar wills. The items bequeathed also offer a fair representation of the type of goods that were valued and considered as heirlooms.

> 'I will and bequethe to my beloved wife Elizabeth my beddsted bedding and all things in my lodginge chamber wholie as it is. Item I geve to my sonne Walter Gasse senior my greatest brasse pott. Item I geve to my sonne Robert Gasse my second great brasse pott. Item I geve my sonne Anthonie Gasse the second greatest brasse panne. Item I geve to my daughter Joane Smart a brasse panne next in greatest to my sonne Anthonie.'

After the bedding and the brass the livestock had to be shared out - as a butcher Alexander Gasse obviously held some fattening fields.

> 'Item I geve to every of my sonnes childerne one ewe sheep apeece also I geve more to John Gasse my sonne Robert's sonne a weanlinge calfe. Item I geve to Samule Gasse my cossen William Gasse's sonne one ewe shepe. Also I geve to the child my daughter Joane now great withall ... one weanlinge calfe.'

94

There are, inevitably, a preponderance of wills made by men because only single women and widows were allowed to make a will: a married woman's possessions essentially belonged to her husband. Nevertheless, it is interesting how many men who pre-deceased their wives chose the wife as sole executrix. Very often the widow had to carry on a family business until her son came of age. This tendency sheds a slightly different light on the economic inter-dependence of the sexes.

Robert and Bettrixe Burnham
Occasionally, the wills of both a man and his widow survive, and these may reveal typically complex family relationships as well as details of worldly possessions. The wills of Robert and Bettrixe Burnham tell a story of family life.

Robert died in 1554, leaving his widow and four daughters very fortunately placed, for his bequests were well above the average. His widow was left a life interest in their dwelling house, which was then to pass to his eldest daughter. Rather impressively, the other three girls each received a house apiece. These four girls, Tomsyn, Elisabeth, Alice and Agnes also received equal interests in 'my great mill called the Town Mill', for Robert Burnham was a miller, probably the first one in the Town Mill after the dissolution and therefore free of the authority of the Abbess, the mill-owner in monastic days.

Robert's daughters also benefited from a selection of domestic items, seemingly a job-lot but presumably carefully chosen by their father. Alice, the third daughter, received 'a table-board lying in the barn and my second flock bed with a bolster, a pair of sheets, a heling [a covering], a

Town Mill shortly before burning down
The timber-framed section in the centre may be the remains of Robert Burnham's mill

95

joined bedsted with a tester of white with a fringe that is in the children's chamber; and my brown cow and my second brass pot, a pan of a bushell, a cupboard that standeth in my buttery, and my table that is in my own chamber with the frame and a joined stool, a coffer that is in the children's chamber, a staved chair and my second brushe, a chafing dish; four ells of white canvas and a candlestick of carnation [pink-coloured]'. Amongst a similar list of goods going to the youngest daughter, Agnes, was his red cow.

Probably the most amusing bequest in Robert Burnham's will came near the end. 'I will my brother Barnes to have my bay colt - if he can be found.' The whereabouts of another colt was equally in doubt.

Bettrixe Burnham died in 1558, four years after her husband. Her will implies that both she and Robert had been married before and that Robert's four daughters were not her children - a common occurrence in those days of short life-spans. Most of Bettrixe's bequests went to her three sons from her previous marriage, confusingly named as Richard Thomas, John Thomas the elder and John Thomas the younger.

The disposal of more practical items may possibly be a link with building material from the monastic precinct - the wording is a little unfortunate to modern ears, but refers to materials in the yard behind her house. Bettrixe left 'to John Hewse two loads of stones in my back-side' and further down 'Item I give and bequeath to my three sons Richard Thomas, John Thomas the Elder and John Thomas the Younger all my stones in my back-side unbequeathed'. At first, with the milling connection, these might be thought of as mill-stones, but there are too many of them - so they may have come from Abbey buildings.

The Poor
Many other fascinating Tudor wills tell of the great stocks of goods held in the workshops of well-to-do inhabitants, or the more modest possessions of the majority of will-makers. It must be remembered, though, that there was a whole underclass that never made a will or left a mark of any sort on history. Only one or two indications of these unfortunates are found in the records. The anonymous vagrant, or lowly servant

for whom no surname was known, has the occasional brief line in the burial records, the numbers of these lost souls in any one year often a potent sign of pitiless weather or failed harvest - or both. Life was still very uncertain.

The straitened circumstances of the unfortunate poor continued to be relieved by the charitable bequests made in wills. Thus, in 1596, Peter Yates left ten shillings to the poor people of Romsey 'the Collectors to have the distribution of it'. By 'the Collectors' he meant those responsible for collecting the Poor Rate introduced during Queen Elizabeth's reign.

It is perhaps indicative of the fledgling state of local government generally that responsibility for the poor devolved on the churchwardens. They worked on behalf of the Select Vestry, an elected committee representing all parishioners, under the auspices of the Overseers of the Poor. In 1563 it was made compulsory for a parish to support its own poor, and this was done by raising a Poor Rate. The Privy Council appointed Justices of the Peace all over the country and they in turn appointed Overseers of the Poor for every parish.

The actual work probably fell mainly on the shoulders of the churchwardens. The workload was increased by a further Act of Parliament in 1572. This required the keeping of a register of the 'Impotent Poor' and the provision of 'a stock of materials necessary for employment of all persons unable to find work and to house them and pay them for their work'. A few years later the 1601 Elizabethan Poor Law Act was an impressive attempt to consolidate and codify the patchwork of legislation that had gone before; England was way ahead of other countries in this effort.

After 1576 the idle and vagrant of Romsey, together with those guilty of minor offences, were sent to a new type of institution, a House of Correction, in Winchester. This building, which cost some £500 to set up, contained 40 beds, each with a flock mattress, bolster, sheets, blankets and a coverlet, with 'some sheets to shift withall'. The working apparatus included looms, tenter-racks and a copper furnace and vats for a dye-house. The unskilled were committed for five years to learn a craft or trade under competent instructors. If numbers failed to reach eighty, the poor could be admitted, on orders from the justices, but not the impotent or diseased. Parents and masters might also apply to have unruly children or idle servants sent to this House of Correction, the parents or masters paying for the service. It must have been an awesome deterrent.

Despite the official framework set up by the justices of the peace through the Overseers of the Poor, some will-makers preferred to place their charitable bequests into mayoral hands for administration, noticeably when leaving land or large sums of money for investment on behalf of the needy. The town council was probably also responsible for the control of begging. An act of 1531 had decreed that deserving paupers could be licensed to beg; twenty years later they were to wear badges in order to bring this recognised activity under the control of the authorities.

The Romsey Mayoralty
It is not easy to define the emerging pattern of civic life during the second half of the 16th century but it clearly evolved around the long established mayoralty in close co-operation with church officials. Only a few names of late 16th-century mayors emerge from the records. William Pratt was one who served in the post-monastic period. He is mentioned in the 1578 will of John Browne, who declared 'I give unto William Pratt now mayor my best sword'. The sword itself was part of John Browne's armoury, which shows him obedient to the need

to be ready to defend the realm when called upon to do so. Other legatees received his 'best bow and the sheaf of arrows', his second sword and his 'harquebus with flask and touchbox'. Not only the local government but the general populace had to be ready for anything in 16th-century Romsey.

Middlebridge Street cottages

THE STUART ERA: The Growth of Civic Independence

As the 17th century began and the Tudor dynasty was replaced by the Stuarts, most Romsey people continued to be engaged in one of the three main areas of work that had dominated the economy since medieval times - agriculture, leather-based trades, or the cloth-finishing industry. The only real exceptions were those engaged in providing the necessities of life - the butcher, the baker and the candle-maker, together with the blacksmith and other essential occupations - and their success was itself dependent on that of the core industries. It was a narrow economic base, but a few made good fortunes, perhaps by becoming employers of home-based piece-workers.

The town probably greeted the 17th century in mixed mood, uncertain whether to be worried or elated by this new start. There was concern about public expenses, especially about the cost of repairing the three-arched stone crossing at Middlebridge, by now in dire straits. Some worried individuals continued to leave bequests towards its repair. On the other hand, bread prices, which had soared during the 1590s, seemed to be settling back again. People must have felt encouraged by this. Perhaps they noticed, too, the very gradual improvement in life-expectancy.

Although some people were living longer, the number of births still did not always outstrip the number of deaths; migration from the countryside probably boosted, or at least sustained, the number of inhabitants overall. One minor downward blip in the population that occurred in the 1630s had nothing to do with sudden deaths but was part of a nation-wide movement. Parson Avery, vicar of Romsey, found that the Church of England was becoming increasingly incompatible with his Puritanical leanings. He could not accept the constraints of the 39 Articles of Religion to which all Anglican priests were expected to adhere. Consequently, in 1634, he led his extended family to the New World, following in the footsteps of the Pilgrim Fathers. His defection must have unsettled some Romsey people, for several other local families followed. John Knight and his family, for example, sailed from Southampton on the 'James' in 1635.

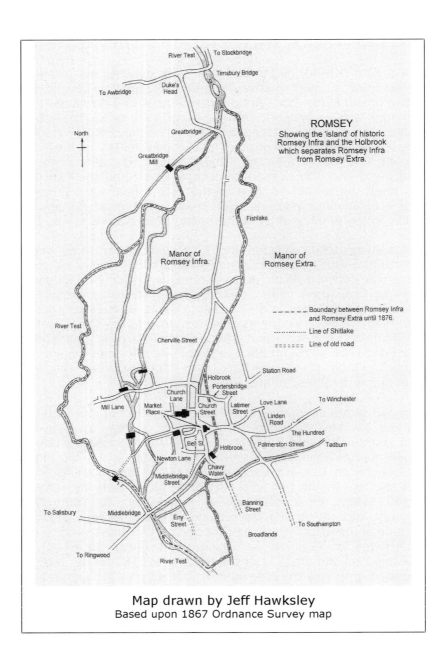

ROMSEY
Showing the 'island' of historic
Romsey Infra and the Holbrook
which separates Romsey Infra
from Romsey Extra.

To Stockbridge
River Test
Timsbury Bridge
To Awbridge
Duke's Head
North
Greatbridge
Greatbridge Mill
Fishlake
Manor of Romsey Infra.
Manor of Romsey Extra.

– – – – – Boundary between Romsey Infra
and Romsey Extra until 1876.
·············· Line of Shitlake
======= Line of old road

River Test
Cherville Street
Station Road
Holbrook
Portersbridge Street
Church Lane
Mill Lane
Market Place
Church Street
Latimer Street
Love Lane
To Winchester
Linden Road
The Hundred
Bell St.
Holbrook
Palmerston Street
Tadburn
Newton Lane
Chavy Water
Middlebridge Street
Banning Street
To Salisbury
Middlebridge
Eny Street
To Southampton
Broadlands
To Ringwood
River Test

Map drawn by Jeff Hawksley
Based upon 1867 Ordnance Survey map

Generally, though, the town must have had an air of stability. Most of the streets still bore a reassuringly familiar Tudor appearance, and several families were laying the foundations of fortunes that would endure for generations. There was an element of determined enterprise and ambition about the town. This manifested itself in the desire to become a borough.

The Borough Charter

1607 was the year in which the first Stuart king, James I, granted a royal charter conferring borough status upon the little township of historic Romsey Infra. That year the king visited Broadlands, where he planted mulberry trees that still survive. His visit must have given extra kudos to Henry St Barbe, who had just succeeded as lord of the manor of Romsey Infra as well as owner of Broadlands, but the new town corporation was determined to strengthen Romsey's growing civic independence. After all, Romsey had joined an elite minority among similar market towns in obtaining borough status. So considerable importance was given to council responsibilities. These ranged from the up-keep of the bull's collar and rope for bull-baiting, to, more acceptably from the modern point of view, the care of the poor. Whilst sharing with the churchwardens the legal obligations of the Elizabethan Poor Law and administering philanthropic endowments, the Corporation also dealt with the matter of discouraging the undeserving poor - the sturdy beggar. A beggar's badge for licensed begging survives from 1678; it features the town's coat of arms.

Although a form of mayoralty had been long established, members of the corporation were anxious to underline the endorsement and authority offered by the royal charter. This had formalised the structure of a mayor, six aldermen, twelve chief burgesses, a town clerk, two sergeants-at-mace and a court recorder, together with the additional right of holding a court, albeit of limited powers. Attention was given to the serious matter of enhancing civic dignity.

Accordingly, a town hall was purchased in 1622. This was adjacent to the north side of the Hundred Bridge and just within the east end of the Market Place. In the western part of the ground floor, the town constable had his office from which he

101

had a commanding view of everyone entering and leaving Romsey Infra across the Hundred Bridge. In the next room, alongside the Holbrook Stream, was the gaol. The mayor and corporation met in the upper room with its own side entrance from the street. In 1672, during the mayoralty of William Kent, the corporation ordered a mace. It cost £10, and still survives today as the lesser mace carried by the junior mace-bearer. It was during the same period that the council chamber was embellished by wooden panels painted with the coats of arms of the high stewards and of the court recorders who had already served the town under the terms of King James' charter. These coats-of-arms have also survived and in recent years have been restored and displayed inside the present town hall.

Romsey's First Town Hall
(now 23 Market Place)
as drawn by Dr John Latham, 1740-1837
Reproduced by permission of The British Library
Shelfmark: BL Mss 26774-26780

Difficult Times

But no-one waved a magic wand over Romsey as the charter was granted, and life was not all plain-sailing as the decades passed. Health became a major concern. Nationally, the upward swing of life-expectancy stalled towards the mid-1600s. It is uncertain how much this negative trend affected Romsey, since poor health in the ever-growing and increasingly unwholesome large cities must have weighted the figures. It is clear, though, that more virulent forms of smallpox and typhus made people increasingly fearful during this period. Even the gentry were not immune from overwhelming epidemics. The St Barbe family suffered a double tragedy in 1656 when husband and wife both died on the same day. Interestingly, their illness was still being described as the 'sweating sickness' of earlier times. The memorial to this sad event may be seen in the south transept of Romsey Abbey.

One widespread disaster that may have had repercussions in Romsey was the famine of 1625. Bad weather resulted in poor crops, and the economy suffered. Again there is little direct evidence of how Romsey fared at this time, but there is a possible indicator in the marriage records. During the early 1600s the annual totals of registered marriages were in the high teens and twenties. During 1625 and 1626 the numbers dropped below ten for each year. And, even when they rose to 15 in 1627, five of the brides were widows (there was never any mention of whether the bridegrooms were widowers). Although these are very raw figures, it does look as if there may have been sound reasons - health or economic reasons - why fewer people were getting married for a while. This situation was not eased by a gradual shift in Romsey's cloth trade, as quality clothwork was replaced by the manufacture of shalloon, a closely woven woollen material mostly used for linings.

The more practical matter of bridge maintenance continued to trouble the inhabitants. After substantial repairs had been made to Middlebridge, at a cost of some £190, the town had to wait for more than another 150 years before it was replaced. In the meantime other bridges, large and small, taxed the town's resources. Greatbridge at the north of town was regularly in disrepair, and was destroyed during the Civil War.

103

The town did, however, succeed in its long held ambition of setting the church bells into the Abbey tower, thus enabling the demolition of the old free-standing parish belfry in the 1620s.

Another concern that Romsey shared with the rest of England was the matter of the Ship Money payments demanded by Charles I. In October 1635 a proclamation was issued to the Constables of the Hundred of King's Somborne that a ship of 600 tonnes should be got ready, and Romsey was assessed in the sum of £30. The amounts that tax-paying inhabitants had to find varied enormously. Thomas Brackley, clothier, was assessed at £1 2s 6d, whereas Alice Parsons, a widow, was only expected to pay 2s 6d. The lowest amount demanded was a shilling. Anyone who refused to pay was liable to have their goods seized, so people complied however unwilling they might be. The money collected was taken to the *Swan Inn*.

The Outside World
Generally, King and Parliament did not seek to interfere with local government during the 17th century, but Romsey was still aware of the outside world. A town crier would regularly proclaim the news, so that the local population heard of declarations of war and peace, victories in battle, celebrations of royal birthdays, coronations, returns to royal health and anything else that could give cause for good cheer or concern. When the Duke of Buckingham was assassinated, his death was recorded in the annals of the town; perhaps the fact that this event took place at Portsmouth brought it closer to home.

At times, too, the inhabitants had to take recourse to higher authorities outside the town. In 1634, a complaint was made by Benjamin Goodwyn to whom Charles I had granted letters patent from the Great Seal for retailing tobacco in the town of Romsey. This was generally a profitable trade; in July 1638, one ounce of tobacco sold for 3d. But Benjamin had problems. He had paid for his licence, but he stated 'that various tradesmen without any licence under the pretence of giving away tobacco do elude the said Letters Patent'. An edict from Whitehall dated 18th September 1634 put matters right thus: 'Any person or persons so offending or being found guilty on examination to be put in gaol unless bond be given with good sureties for due obedience in future'.

The Civil War

Disputes apart, local wills suggest that the town maintained its commercial success. By the mid-17th century, urban Romsey was essentially a solid business community in which several family dynasties were beginning to evolve. The Gasse family, for example, descendants of the Tudor butcher, Alexander Gasse, were continuing in the family trade, and would do so for much of the 18th century as well. It was the sort of enterprising setting in which the new Puritan ideas might be favourably received; Romsey must have already been impressed by the example of Parson Avery, his family and followers.

It is difficult, though, to gauge the attitude of the townspeople at the outbreak of the Civil War. The St Barbes of Broadlands, along with many gentry in the south-east, are said to have favoured the Parliamentary side, losing one son as the result of wounds received at the first Battle of Newbury in 1643. There is an inkling that Romsey, too, favoured Parliament, but it is likely that the town was simply anxious for peace. By the time the town had been subjected to several skirmishes and plundered by both sides, a sense of general ill-usage must have been uppermost.

Some deaths amongst the soldiers must have added to the unease. On 12th December 1643 five were buried 'all slain at the routing of the King's forces at Romsey'. On 6th February 1644 Richard Gold, a soldier, was slain by his own musket, apparently an accident. In May 1644 two Roundhead soldiers were hanged, by their own side, outside the *Swan Inn*.

Urged on from the pulpit by the rantings of a Puritanical cleric, soldiers destroyed much of the internal fabric of the Abbey, an act of desecration or cleansing according to opposing views of how churches should look and how services should be conducted. Altogether, it must have been a very unsettling and worrying time.

Romsey's concern about destruction and plundering in the town surfaced at the Hampshire Assizes in 1647. The townspeople sought permission to raise money for the repair of Great Bridge, 'taken downe by officers under command of General

Norton upon urgent occasions and now greatly decayed'. Crossing the River Test in and out of either end of Romsey was not easy.

In late 1648 Charles I must have crossed Middlebridge as he passed through Romsey on his way from Hurst Castle to London after captivity on the Isle of Wight. No mention has survived of how people felt about his ultimate fate, and the Cromwellian Interregnum that followed had little noticeable impact on Romsey. One or two records refer to the 'Lord Protector' but generally the town carried on as before. In Church Street, the town property of the manor of South Wells was temporarily removed from the ownership of the Dean and Canons of St George's Chapel, Windsor, one of the royal chantries dissolved under Cromwell and restored by Charles II. It is doubtful if this had any great effect on the tenants, who simply continued paying rent to the intermediate lessees of the whole manor.

The Restoration and New Religion

Behind this Church Street facade lies the timber-framed home of John Cox, shoemaker, the mayor of Romsey at the Restoration of Charles II in 1660

Whatever their opinions, most Romsey people were ready in 1660 to take their oath of allegiance to the newly restored Charles II. The first to take the oath was the mayor, who in that year was John Cox, a shoemaker. His timber-framed

106

house is now occupied by the *Oasis Christian Centre* at No 25 Church Street.

Within a couple of years, however, there was considerable heart-searching among many local people when the Clarendon Code made it difficult for those of a Nonconformist persuasion to remain within the Church of England. The broad church of the Interregnum was no more.

It is no accident, therefore, that the foundation date outside the United Reformed Church - 'the Church by the Arch' - is 1662, this being the date when the church was founded, not when the present building was put up. Groups of Independents and Presbyterians gained ground in late 17th-century Romsey. Two clerics, John and Thomas Warren, were the leading lights of this new Puritanical

Memorial stone by doorway of the United Reformed Church, Romsey

It reads: *This memorial stone was laid by James Spicer JP DL on the 7th day of September 1886 on behalf of the Congregational Church founded by the Rev. Thomas Warren MA formerly Rector of Houghton in this County AD1662*

religion within the town. Their movement evolved into the Independent Chapel, later known as the Congregational Church and now the United Reformed Church. One of the best known early members of the local congregation was Richard Cromwell, popularly known as 'Tumbledown Dick'. He was the son of Oliver Cromwell, and travelled some five miles from Hursley Manor, having married the daughter of the house there.

Another national parish survey, the Compton Census, was taken in 1676. This supports the view that the dissenting groups and Romsey's overall population had started to grow again, though the parish records indicate troughs in the generally upward curve. Writing some five years later, the respected 17th-century economist, Sir William Petty, who was born in Romsey, commented that he considered 'the Bishops late Numbring of the Communicants' correlated satisfactorily with figures suggested by the Poll Tax and the Hearth Tax.

The Compton Census claimed, rather astonishingly, that Romsey had, by 1676, no fewer than 777 non-communicants, though still only three Papists. Amongst those designated as non-communicants may have been the slackers and non-believers, but, even allowing for these, the Nonconformists must have been flourishing in a population of about 2,500. Whether this increased support for the dissenting faith was due to a long-held preference for Puritanical ideals, or the influence of charismatic leaders like the Warrens, is impossible to tell.

Successful Citizens

In terms of the economy, the woollen cloth trade continued to thrive throughout the 17th century. There were woolcombers, spinners and weavers in the town, but the big money remained in the finishing of the cloth and dealing in it. Some individuals made good fortunes. When the clothier Richard Puckeridge died intestate in 1672, his widow felt justified in presenting the administrators of his estate with a £50 bill for funeral expenses, an enormous sum for the time.

But it was the son of a fairly modest dyer who probably made the biggest impact in the long run. William Petty was born in 1623 in a large half-timbered house on the west side of Church Street, roughly where Nos 28 and 30 now stand. He was destined to become the economist, Sir William Petty - also founder member of the Royal Society and a true polymath; he was a highly esteemed ancestor of the Marquess of Lansdowne.

Perhaps Sir William Petty lacked public charisma, for he never acquired the popular renown of some of his contemporaries, but he was a fascinating character, highly respected in many fields. Somehow he managed to work for Cromwell and gain favour with Charles II, who knighted him. Amongst other things he practised anatomy; he developed many inventions including a working catamaran; he devised and supervised a mapping system for Ireland; and he had very forward-thinking ideas about the economy and education. He believed in the intrinsic value of education for all, including girls, and left charitable bequests for the education of Romsey children.

Another 17th-century charity was set up in the 1690s by John Kent. After an impoverished childhood, he made a fortune as a silk-thrower in London. In recognition of the support he had received as a child from a kindly Romsey neighbour, he endowed four almshouses for widows in Middlebridge Street. Modern replacements are still in use on the same site.

Crime and Punishment

Less worthy inhabitants were treated to the traditional punishments of the time - whipping, pillory, stocks, ducking or fines. More brutal punishments were reserved for those committing the greater crimes. There were severe penalties for an unsavoury pair of murderers, Esther Ives and her lover, John Noyse. She lived in Romsey with her husband, William Ives. Her lover, who was 'by Trade a Cooper but a person of ill Fame and a very Desolute Liver', came from nearby Wellow village.

The Ives kept a 'victualling house', and there, on 5th February 1686, John Noyse stayed drinking until the early hours of the morning. He and Esther then murdered William Ives in his bed 'to make a freer way for their unlawful lust'. Esther, rather unwisely, told their children that their father was dead; they 'fell into loud lamentations', at which point they were overheard by the nightwatchman on his rounds. He was alarmed, having heard John Ives cry out 'What dost thou do to me, Noyse?' shortly before. He therefore alerted the Constable of the Watch who arrived on the scene with a guard, just in time to catch the guilty pair in the act of dressing the body of John Ives preparatory to despatching him down the stairs in an attempt to make his murder look like an accident. The Constable did not need to be much of a detective. Upon finding a bloodstained pillow and blood all over Esther, he charged the pair and they were committed to Romsey gaol.

There they stayed until the Lenten Assizes in Winchester, where John Noyse was sentenced to be hanged and Esther Ives to be burnt at the stake. On 11th March, they were taken from Winchester to Romsey, 'placed upon one Horse'. Back in

Romsey, John Noyse was publicly hanged. Esther Ives was tied to the stake, and the fuel placed around her to die the death of an adulterous murdering wife. However, by a discretionary concession recognised by authorities generally, the executioner strangled her first. Then, 'the Fire was kindled and she consumed to Ashes'. The place of these executions is unknown, though Dr John Latham, writing from hearsay over a century later, declared it to be the Market Place.

The Poor

Treatment of the poor changed during this century. After the Winchester House of Correction had been going for some fifty years, the authorities began to use it in a different way. On the whole, only vagrants of a desperate and violent nature were committed to Winchester, whilst workhouses were set up locally for the more unfortunate.

Romsey Infra and Romsey Extra each had a workhouse. The Overseers usually rented buildings on a yearly basis, and the locations moved about over time so that it cannot be said with any certainty where they were. It seems, though, that the need for such establishments was understood and tolerated without too much stigma attached. As the century progressed, more refinements were added to the administration of the Poor Law, particularly the law of settlement and removal. This compelled any poor person travelling in search of work to carry a certificate from his parish of origin stating that his home parish accepted liability for him. Without such a certificate the poor would not be welcome in another parish, a procedure that was to be heavily and harshly used in the 18th century.

Romsey Market

The market, once the province of the Abbess's Steward, was now under purely secular control. The 1607 charter had designated the mayor as clerk of the market, while the rights and profits of the market continued to go to the lord of the manor. The one surviving document about the Romsey market and fairs was drawn up in 1696. It is not very informative, containing only a list of charges. But it does imply that some areas were almost run as small franchises within the main market, noticeably the shoemakers' section.

Apart from farm animals for sale, the market was bustling every week with stall-holders who ranged from butchers to bodice makers [corset makers], and included cutlers, tobacconists, gardeners, pedlars, hawkers, edge-tool makers, weavers and bakers plus a glover, a hosier and a soap-boiler.

Intriguingly, the market stall list included a mountebank's stage. A mountebank is defined as 'an itinerant quack who from an elevated platform appealed to his audience by means of stories, tricks, juggling, and the like, in which he was often assisted by a professional clown or fool' [OED]. He seems a more likely figure for the fairs than for a weekly market but perhaps the market customers were very gullible or desperate about their health.

End of the Century
Just to re-inforce the civic awareness that was such an important part of this century, the town received a confirmation charter from William III in 1695. This endorsed the 1607 charter of James I and made one or two minor adjustments to it, notably to the powers of the court.

And so the 17th century ended. In the 18th century Romsey was obliged, along with other communities, to start looking increasingly outwards, and, more significantly for the individual, to start thinking of new ways of making a living.

Watercolour of Romsey Market Place, 1809
by unknown artist
showing the side rails of the Hundred Bridge in the foreground
Reproduced by kind permission of the University of Southampton
Reference: Cope Collection cq ROM 91.5 MAR
[cover picture]

THE GEORGIAN PERIOD: Economic Upheaval

1700-1714 - The Last of the Stuarts

The last decades of the Stuart dynasty must have seemed promising in Romsey, even exciting. As the 18th century began, noticeable changes could be seen in the Market Place, where timber-framed houses along the west side were already being replaced by quietly elegant brick buildings.

These new houses probably occupied the same ground area as their predecessors, but, by soaring a further storey than most of them, and by providing sturdy brick inner walls and cellars, they offered spaciousness and privacy to the favoured few, together with a level of comfort never experienced before. The lofty scale of the rooms with large sash windows and the latest fireplaces must have impressed those who visited the owners of these new homes.

From their rear windows the proud occupants might have been the first to see the Abbey clock, said to have been placed on the tower in 1725. Whether people relied on the clock is another matter, since it seems to have been a poor time-keeper, while the chimes were so unreliable that they were eventually left out of repair in the 1790s and removed altogether in 1800.

In the early 1700s a few other new houses appeared on the outskirts of town, at locations where the owners could obtain larger sites with pleasure grounds. Around most of the streets, some older houses acquired smart new facades; tiles began to replace thatch; open shop fronts were enclosed behind windows and shopkeepers retreated

Wykeham House, The Hundred

upstairs to comfortable quarters 'over the shop'. The style of Romsey was changing.

End of an Economic Era

At first, there were few obvious signs that the basic economy of the town was also under threat of change. The leather-based trades still featured skinning, tanning, the dyeing and dressing of leather, shoemaking, glove-making, and the production of ever-important agricultural items, such as saddles and horse collars. Romsey's Cheese Fairs reflected the continued importance of agriculture and of dairy produce in particular.

Amongst the better-off inhabitants there were still affluent clothiers to invest in some of the new fashions. They were numerous enough to make the local inhabitants comfortable about the continuing success of the woollen-cloth trade that had sustained the town's economy since the Middle Ages. They included men such as Edward Hunt, John Storke and John Gifford, who each became mayor of Romsey. The cloth-finishing and wool-dealing trades may have changed style - especially with the introduction of shalloon manufacture - but they continued to give work to a high proportion of the local population, with craftsmen undertaking woolcombing, weaving, fulling, dyeing, nap-shearing and similar related activities.

It was a dangerously high proportion. As the Georgian era began, the whole local economy was delicately balanced on the success of activities related to woollen-cloth, leather and agriculture. The failure of just one of them could plunge the neighbourhood into depression. Nevertheless, the inhabitants of Romsey had adapted to changes of emphasis, such as the production of lower quality shalloon cloth, and having seen relative prosperity in the preceding decades, they assumed it would continue into the 18th century.

Ahead, though, loomed one of the most difficult times for many small market towns of southern England, and Romsey was no exception. New building slowed perceptibly; only a few properties can be positively identified for the period of George I and George II, and only a few bricklayers featured in 18th-century Romsey before the 1740s. Those who were bricklayers probably made their money more from infilling timber-framed buildings with brick, where wattle and daub had sufficed before, or by giving old properties new facades, rather than from erecting totally new buildings.

The beginning of the 18th century marked a transitional hiatus, not clearly seen at the time, between an old economy and a new one. There had been changes in life-style over the previous centuries, but they were as nothing compared with the economic upheaval that Romsey was to experience over the next fifty years. The old timeless work pattern was severely undermined.

Nationally, there were crop failures during the opening decade of the 18th century, with bread prices soaring in 1708 and 1709. More profoundly, a fashion for new fabrics began to threaten the manufacture of woollen cloth, and later the emergence of coal-driven steam power gradually drew the focus of industry towards the northern coalfields. Although many Romsey individuals were still classified as clothiers, they were not operating on the scale of their predecessors, nor succeeding so well.

Known Romsey Workforce in occupations related to agriculture or the cloth and leather industries		
17th century	18th century	early 19th century
340 out of 520 known names	307 out of 930 known names	120 out of 625 known names

A table showing the diminishing dependence on the core occupations that had dominated medieval and early modern Romsey. Some of the later fall in numbers reflects larger units of operation, especially in agriculture.

A superficial look at the work being carried out by the workers of urban Romsey throughout the 18th century would suggest that the woollen-cloth trade continued to flourish. Various records show that there were still many who proudly called themselves clothiers.

Nevertheless, there were differences. The proportion of inhabitants linked to the cloth industry had fallen, and the word 'clothier' had itself changed meaning. In the 17th century it had indicated a man with a wool-loft full of many different coloured cloths and yarns - and even probably employees or out-workers. In the 18th century the term came to be used much more loosely, so that it often described, for example, a woolcomber, who simply prepared the basic wool for the spinner. Many of the weavers were apparently reduced to weaving sacks, whilst, with only one known exception, the dyers failed to survive into the 18th century. Although a few cloth dealers continued well into the 19th century, the trade was no longer the mainstay of Romsey's prosperity. As the cloth trade shrank there was distress in Romsey during the early decades of the 18th century, for no new occupations evolved in its place, or, like paper-making, were still in very early stages. Many people were reduced to poverty.

Treatment of the Poor

Overall responsibility for the poor continued to be the duty of the parish officials, as laid down by Act of Parliament. Essentially, the law divided the poor into three categories: those without work, for whom a poorhouse or workhouse should be set up, complete with suitable materials for work; those who were able but refused to work, who were sent to a House of Correction where they could be taught a trade; and those who were unable to work, for whom almshouses should be provided.

Throughout the Georgian period, as before, it was generally, if grudgingly, accepted that communities should raise rates for the welfare of their poor. Probably a fifth of the 18th-century population came within this category, perhaps more at certain periods. The demands on the Poor Rate must have placed considerable strain on the indulgence of the more affluent, but there was still no great disgrace attached to those who fell, perhaps only temporarily, on hard times. In fact, even the poorest were given rights, and could appeal at the Quarter Sessions if they thought they were being unfairly treated.

The Law of Settlement

The procedure that must have caused greatest heartache to the poor was that related to 'settlements'. Settlement in a parish was acquired by renting a property of more than £10 per annum, paying rates, working as a servant for over a year, or serving an apprenticeship. If none of these qualifications applied, the settlement was the place of a person's birth. Women and children took their husbands' or fathers' settlement. An impoverished widow might be forced to leave her own family and go to her late husband's birthplace, which she might never have visited before. This harsh system was devised to avoid the problem of parishes, particularly town parishes, suffering an influx of needy people who might overwhelm local resources.

Romsey magistrates attended the hearings of hundreds of settlement cases during the 17th and 18th centuries. A great deal of time and money was taken by parish officers in ensuring that relief was given only to those for whom they were legally responsible. Sometimes, parishes appealed at Quarter Sessions against the decisions made by local magistrates and, in Hampshire, counsels were employed to plead their cases.

Most cases, though, were settled at the local level. Between 1681 and 1783, the sparsely populated Romsey Extra alone dealt with 181 cases, of which 28 claimants proved to belong to Romsey Infra. There were several men listed as serge weavers, indicating the slow demise of the local cloth trade. The more crowded urban area of Romsey Infra carried out about 150 examinations of applicants for poor relief between 1791 and 1808. Each was signed by the magistrates and the applicant, though the latter, particularly if a woman, could often only manage a cross.

An Orphan Family

Among the Quarter Sessions records is the sad story of some orphans. In 1700, the parish of St Laurence in Southampton appealed for the removal of some orphan children. Seven years earlier their father, Hugh Reeves, a cooper by trade, had been living in Romsey Extra when he was impressed to work in the Kings Yard at Southampton. He brought his wife, Mary, and his children to Southampton with him. Hugh worked for some years but became sick and died, leaving Mary and their children. Mary then died. The court decided the children should be removed to the care of the Overseers of the Poor of Romsey Extra.

Paying for the Poor

No one ever enjoyed paying rates or collecting them. In Romsey, as elsewhere, the basis for the system seems to have been fair. Rates were assessed on land, buildings (including stables and barns), stocks of goods, and tithes. Dr John Latham, writing about Romsey in the early 1800s, explained that the rateable value of a property was based on the rent. Each year the Select Vestry met and decided on a rate for the ensuing year. This had to be approved by the Justices of the Peace. A very full list of ratepayers for Romsey Infra, divided into the three tythings, survives from 1745. There were over three hundred assessments, the highest 5s 0d for a paper mill and the lowest ½d for a garden. The total collected was £6 15s 4½d.

The actual care of those receiving support was handed over as a business enterprise. Local businessmen were invited to tender 'to lodge, keep, maintain and employ' the poor in the workhouse for a fixed amount per head for one year or longer, a difficult challenge. Rising costs caused Mr Watts and Mr Withers to ask to be discharged from their agreements in 1793. In 1798, the lowest comprehensive tender, £796 per annum, was made by Thomas Meredith. Two years later, in 1800, he was paid extra to cover increased costs. As this was a time when bread prices soared astronomically - doubling the 1798 price - it is unlikely that the poor were suddenly receiving better treatment.

Bequests and Endowments for the Poor
Charitable bequests still played an important part in relieving the lot of the poor. Thomas Shory was a friend of the same John Kent who had set up Kent's Almshouses in the 1690s. In 1703, Thomas Shory gave 'a piece of ground in a common field called Abbotswood at Romsey' to the Mayor and Corporation. The rent was to be distributed by the Mayor and the Vicar to poor communicants on Thursday in Trinity Week.

In 1718 John Nowes left a large property at Lee, to the south of Romsey. He arranged for the rents and profits to be used for the schooling, clothing and apprenticing of 40 poor boys, 20 of them to be from Romsey. Five years later, Sir John St Barbe of Broadlands made a similar educational bequest. The motives behind such educational endowments - which were becoming increasingly popular nationwide - may not always have been as altruistic as those professed by Sir William Petty. Many amongst the gentry were fearful that a discontented poor might recreate the scenario that had resulted in the Civil War. Nevertheless, Romsey's poor did benefit from the philanthropy of some better-off inhabitants.

Poor Children
Many poor Romsey children were apprenticed over the years, a promising policy which could benefit all parties. The process involved the Overseers in an initial expenditure, but meant that the child ceased to be a charge on the parish, as the master would assume responsibility for the child. In the years between 1683 and 1783 the Vestry Books listed 185 poor children in Romsey Extra who were apprenticed.

Other employment was found for a few children. Spinning and quilling - the practice of winding spun thread on to quills, or reeds, ready for weaving - were convenient, because they were both cottage industries requiring little in the way of apparatus.

Bastardy Bonds
Bastard children were invariably so described in the Baptismal Registers. Although no stigma attached before Victorian times, illegitimacy was not very common until the 17th century. By the middle of the 18th century, however, the numbers had soared. This change in mores may have been partly, though not wholly, prompted by a higher level of poverty that left many young people unable to find homes or employment before embarking on marriage. Undoubtedly, the Overseers of the Poor struggled to support destitute mothers and children.

The government stepped in to help the Overseers by introducing the official system of Bastardy Bonds. By such a bond the father agreed with the parish Overseers that he would be responsible for the child. In a book containing the records of the Parish of Romsey Extra, details of Bastardy Bonds are entered between the years 1700 and 1780. Some cases show the father to be a labourer, but at the other end of the social scale, some were described as 'Gent'. Regardless of status, some bond-makers had endorsements from family members to make their bond more secure. In 1764 Joseph James and Hugh James, both of Romsey Extra, one a butcher and the other described as 'yeoman', agreed 'to indemnify the parish against a male bastard child of Martha Hewlett'.

Outrelief for the Poor
Outrelief was the means of support for those in need but not so desperate that they had to enter the workhouse. By the middle

119

of the 18th century, it was noted that the Churchwardens, Overseers and principal inhabitants were 'oppressed with numerous poor persons by which means great inconveniency and troubles happen to Overseers'. A committee was formed to support the Churchwardens in hearing applications and complaints from the poor, and this system was continued by the Board of Guardians, which took over care of the poor after 1835.

Many applications were for shoes and clothes. Most applications for shoes were allowed, as were some requests for clothes, but most requests for coats were refused. Families were given 'changes of lining' [linen] for their children but the items of clothing were not specified. Rents were generally refused on the basis that landlords were abusing the system.

Some needed help with health problems. 'Cheeseman and children' wanted their heads cured of scurvy, which was allowed, and Widow New was able to send her child to the Hampshire County Hospital at Winchester, to which Romsey Extra paid a yearly contribution. John Godfrey wanted his girls to be put out to service, and the committee agreed.

Help was sometimes granted to enable the poor to become self-supporting. John Brockman was given 20s 0d to buy leather to enable him to work. Hannah Bennet was allowed 'a spinning turn and jack to go out of the workhouse'. Others, in contrast, applied to go into the workhouse or, preferably, an almshouse.

Dr John Bartlett died in 1815, having endowed almshouses to bear his name. The Bartlett Almshouses, giving shelter to eight needy women, were built at the south-west end of Middlebridge Street, but had to be pulled down in the 1930s, when the new by-pass was routed through the original site.

The Dissenters

In these difficult times many were receptive to the dissenting views of the new religious groups evolving in Romsey. The Baptists, particularly, touched a chord amongst the poor and those concerned about their welfare. The present-day Baptist church traces its lineage back to 1750, but there is evidence of Anabaptists in the town by 1715, though a link with this earlier group is uncertain. Meeting in Middlebridge Street and baptising their adult members in the Holbrook Stream, the Baptists found their greatest support in the surrounding area. Towards the end of the century a group of Quakers had a meeting house at the north end of Narrow Lane, just off Abbey Water.

Law and Order
Despite the hard times endured by so many of the inhabitants, 18th-century Romsey seems not to have been a hot-bed of crime - there was nothing to compare with the murder of William Ives. Nevertheless, law and order had to be maintained. In 1735 there was a sharp reminder in the Court Leet records that a ducking stool and stocks should be provided.

Some offences were of a civil nature. In 1737 John Light was indicted before the quarter sessions and found guilty of trading as a barber for five months contrary to statute. He was fined £6, which seems a lot, though barbers were also 'surgeons' at that time - so he may have had a good income. In 1739 Elizabeth Crowther was sent to the House of Correction (in Winchester) for giving birth to a bastard child and refusing to name the father.

In the same year James Bowner was whipped in the Market Place for stealing two sacks valued at 6d and two bushels of bran valued at 4d. Swift and visible justice was important so that traders and their customers could feel that their goods were as secure as possible. 1743 saw two women whipped from Cherville Street to the Market Place for petty larceny, a theft of goods under 12d in value. They may have considered themselves lucky, as the option of transportation had been introduced by this date. Thomas Newman suffered a double punishment in 1746 - he was committed to the House of Correction and was whipped for stealing a hen worth 6d.

The borough tried to keep an eye on its punishment tools. A cat-o-nine-tails was bought for 6d in 1751. Then in 1765 the stocks were reported to be 'out of repair' and the Clerk of the Market was rebuked for not having a whipping post in the Market Place. Perhaps the sorry state of the stocks and absence of a whipping post indicated that there was little use for them.

There certainly seems to have been a slow change in the public's view of cruel spectacles, whether punishment or entertainment. Bull-baiting, support of which had cost the Corporation considerable sums of money over the decades, came to an end in the 18th century. The town hall accounts had regularly quoted substantial costs for repairing ropes and replacing collars for the bull. The bull-baiting was long enjoyed by the populace and appreciated by the butchers who profited by it. The baiting was said to make tough meat tender and so more attractive to customers. More enlightened views won the day, however, and in 1789 the practice was ended by law. The bull had got its own back by 'getting loose and running down streets injuring some and frightening many'. Local butchers protested at the ban and took their case to Winchester, but wiser counsel again prevailed and the case was not publicly heard. The cost of the case was said to have ruined some of the complainants.

In fact the butchers had suffered other trouble in 1787, when the Beast Market at Salisbury raised a toll to pay for a new Council House. Romsey butchers were enraged and resolved to form their own local market on a field called Periton behind the *Queen's Head Inn* (on an area now occupied by the bus station and adjacent car-parks). To celebrate this exciting development, a bull was paraded through Romsey with gilded horns and wearing a notice that read 'No Toll for Romsey Forever', after which the poor beast met with a swift demise and was roasted whole. No doubt the approving populace fell to with a will. After a few months Salisbury Corporation saw the error of its ways and cancelled the toll. The market returned to Salisbury with only a small livestock market continuing in Romsey.

Other losers were the enthusiasts for cock-fighting. There was a particular Romsey tradition for tormenting cocks on Shrove Tuesday. 'On Shrove Tuesday at 12 o'clock a knell is tolled for an hour on the Great Bell at Romsey called the Cock's Knell'. Dr Latham recorded what he had been told about this event.

122

'I am glad to find no traces in Romsey of the remains of another cruel sport viz. throwing at cockes on Shrove Tuesday. Known here by the name of Cock Skailing I suspect it was discontinued about 1752 as I find in the Corporation accounts the following items: For postage of Proclamation and crying down cock scailing 9s.0d.

For it is not only not now used ...... but not remembered by any middle aged persons. Before this time the practice used to be in every avenue round the old Market House to a great annoyance of all; the aggressors were first driven off into bye places especially beyond Great Bridge and being tired out at last left off so cruel a custom so completely as to have no traces left.'

Success for Some

As is always the case, there were exceptions within the general pattern of a poor economy. Among the successful or secure people in Romsey and the surrounding countryside in the early 1700s, it was fortunate that there were a few who looked with concern upon the increasing number of desperate poor.

Although the Romsey paper-making industry was in its infancy in the early 1700s, John Hockley achieved considerable success with his paper-mill at Rivermead. It may have started at the end of the 17th century, and was certainly in operation by the beginning of the next. In 1745 Mr Hockley's business was carrying the highest assessment for the Poor Tax within the Market Place tything - but Rivermead was the only paper-mill in the town for some time. Many people struggled to make a living, and the ultimate failure of the cloth trade was not easily forgotten. When Dr Latham was recording the town's history in the early 1800s, many still lamented a time when, they claimed, 'a thousand hands had worked the looms'.

While the town generally was in this uncertain state, there must have been a stir when Broadlands changed hands in 1736, the only time it has been on the open market as a private estate. The philanthropic Sir John St Barbe had bequeathed the estate to Sir Henry Sydenham, who leased it to a farmer. For a decade or more the property reverted to its original use as farmlands, and the house was allowed to deteriorate. Then, in 1736, Sir Henry sold Broadlands, thereby breaking a last curious link with the days of the Abbey. The St Barbes had been descendants of the last Abbey Steward, John Foster, and his wife, Jane Wadham, the erstwhile nun. Their daughter, also named Jane, had married William Fleming of Broadlands; their daughter and heiress had, in turn, married into the St Barbe family.

Broadlands' new owner was the first Lord Palmerston, who quickly made an impact on the townscape of Romsey by building an Audit House in the Market Place - more or less where his great-grandson's statue now stands. It was completed at a cost £534 19s 6d.

The Audit House, built 1744
by permission of The British Library
Shelfmark: BL Mss 267774-16780

The Audit House provided space for a limited covered market and a meeting room above. This room was able to serve several purposes – manorial matters could be dealt with there, and the corporation began to look on it as their new town hall. References appear for the 'old town hall'. Perhaps it was the setting in 1746 for the 'treat' on which the Corporation spent £2 5s 0d in celebration of victory at the Battle of Culloden, where the Jacobite rebellion was finally ended. This was one of the many occasions on which the mayor used the annual allocation to be spent on wine, beer and tobacco for loyal demonstrations.

The Audit House may also have been the location of a recruiting office in 1745, when the Corporation was appealing for men to serve in HM Regiment of Foot in Flanders, Menorca, Gibraltar and the Plantations; there is no record of how many signed up. So there was a dual use of this building by the old feudal manor and the still comparatively new corporate borough.

124

Changing Fortunes: The Arrival of the Turnpike Roads

The focus of many events, the Audit House was one of the few noteworthy buildings to be erected in the early Georgian era after the spurt at the end of the Stuart period. The general absence of other new building was part of the malaise that affected Romsey between the 1720s and 1750s.

The upswing, when it came, again followed a wider trend. Improved transport was the key that unlocked Romsey's economy in the mid-18th century. During the 1750s and 1760s, Romsey's position at the hub of a network of major road links was suddenly enhanced by the creation of turnpike roads. These improved roads were financed by trusts whose members took the profits from tolls charged at the turnpike gates as the return on their investments. The most important of these roads led to Southampton, Salisbury and Winchester but others connected to Ringwood, Stockbridge and Botley with Portsmouth beyond.

Although these improved roads were often superimposed on existing routes, new sections were cut for some turnpikes. The medieval way to Salisbury via Greatbridge and Awbridge, for example, was superseded by a new link via Middlebridge and Green Hill; it became part of the major Southampton-Salisbury turnpike. Beyond the new turning to Salisbury, the way over Pauncefoot Hill towards the New Forest developed as the Ringwood turnpike, whilst the old route north through Greatbridge was up-graded as the Stockbridge turnpike. The major route from Romsey to Winchester no longer meandered via Cupernham with a loop back through Jermyns Lane to Ampfield. Instead it carved its way directly and purposefully through Abbotswood along the present-day A3090.

The new roads enormously improved both local and long-distance travel as well as goods transport. Toll houses punctuated significant access points on the edge of town. Within a new pattern of work, they provided a living for local men, as well as a return for investors. *The Hampshire Chronicle* of 13th February 1804 carried an announcement about the 'Turnpike from West Gate of Winchester to the town of Romsey and from thence to the river at Swathling'. It continued 'Tolls will be let by auction at Kings Head Inn,

Hursley, on Monday 12 March between 10am and 12 for one year from 5 April next ..... February 7 1804'.

Smoother road surfaces, often over more straightforward routes, well-placed staging posts where horses could be changed, and improved carriage design, all helped to reduce travelling time. Journeys were accomplished twice as fast as hitherto, and this improvement continued. As a result, travelling became much more popular, with public coaches multiplying as a service. The amount of traffic, public and private, increased beyond all expectations and provided many new work opportunities.

18th-century Romsey began to thrive as a coaching town, and its market hinterland was enlarged by the ease and speed of travel. Access to a wider market enabled brewing, long the province of individual innkeepers, to develop as a major enterprise; large-scale 'common brewers' became significant members of the town's trade and industry elite. They began to buy up their own local chains of public houses to ensure steady sale of their wholesale beer in the growing neighbourhood. Many of Romsey's inns and taverns may be dated to the mid-18th century, some only aiming at local trade but others more ambitiously seeking to satisfy a wider travelling public. Increasingly, the common brewers also acted as spirit and wine agents, buying large quantities at favourable prices from London merchants.

Customers for these commodities were found amongst an increasingly affluent population as an influx of professional men - doctors, lawyers and bankers - created a new upper echelon in Romsey society. In turn they created a market for the fashions of the day; peruke-makers mantua-makers, tea-dealers and other semi-exotic and high-quality occupations became part of Romsey's trading community. Moving away from its manufacturing past, Romsey became the focus for a service industry offering a wide range of goods for the local community and support for a variety of long-distance travellers.

The long-established *White Horse* in the Market Place dominated as the coaching inn for public transport, but the *Bell Inn* in Bell Street held the Royal Mail contract in the 1800s.

NEW & GROWTH OCCUPATIONS: 1750-1837

Occupation	Late 18th C	Early 19th C
Apothecary	4	2
Attorney/Solicitor	3 + clerks	13 + clerks
Auctioneer	1	9
Banker	2	7
Bookseller	1	4
Brewer	20	10
Brickmaker/burner	3	2
Bricklayer [NB: 1 only found for 17th century]	15	14
Cabinet Maker	3	7
Carrier	2	10
China/Glass dealer	1	3
Chymist/Druggist	1	2
Coachmaker	3	3
Coal Merchant		6
Common Brewer	6	4
Confectioner	2	3
Corn Factor	5	8
Dairyman	4	1
Draper	2	11
Fruiterer		2
Gatekeeper/Toll Collector	1	2
Grocer-Tea Dealer [more ordinary grocers besides]	3	13
Hair Dresser	2	5
Hatter	2	2
Innkeepers [only 10 for 17th century]	52	45
Ironmonger	5	6
Maltster [only 3 found in 17th century]	18	17
Milliner/Dressmaker	4	9
Painter/Plumber & Glazier	9	10
Papermaker	16	16
Peruke Maker	10	1
Sack Manufacturer	7	3
Singing Teacher	1	
Shopkeeper/Dealer in Sundries	11	27
Stationer	2	3
Staymaker	1	2
Surgeon	4	8
Watch & Clock Maker	1	2
Whitesmith	4	2
Wine Merchant	3	5

This inn prospered so well in the 18th century that it superimposed its name on historic Mill Street. Other street names changed for less obvious reasons. Cherville Street temporarily became Cox Street, in part at least, while the 'dog-leg' section towards the town centre began to be called by its present name, The Horsefair. Newton Lane was known as Hog Lane for a while. Meanwhile, *The Queen's Head* in The Hundred and *The Swan* and *The Dolphin* in the Market Place also offered posting facilities, all striving to attract private coaches.

The newly sophisticated travelling public required reliable hostelries that in turn needed cooks, chambermaids, ostlers, grooms and serving men. A more elite stratum in local society expected specialist crafts to support their more indulgent life-style. The public service industry had arrived.

Oddly enough, though, the town still seems to have dragged its feet about the up-keep of internal roads and bridges. It might be thought that the better-off inhabitants and the members of the turnpike trusts would have demanded and obtained a higher standard of maintenance than actually pertained. Whatever efforts were made, the records of Romsey's Court Leet indicate their failures. These records contain a litany of despair about unscoured streams, broken bridges and roadways blocked by dung heaps. Even the major bridges suffered, though Middlebridge was rebuilt in the early 1780s. There was also a familiar age-old problem in the form of much passing of responsibility between county authorities, local authorities and the lord of the manor. In some ways Romsey seems to have prospered in spite of itself. In common with the rest of the country the population of Romsey grew.

The rebuilding of Middlebridge
Middlebridge was eventually rebuilt with an elegant single span nearly thirty years after the turnpikes were established. The appearance of the new bridge was a potent symbol of economic rejuvenation. The archaic three-arched bridge that had served so valiantly since medieval times was as broken down as the old work structure. The two piers in deep water were subject to the swirling violence of the river currents that they entrapped. Both were leaning, but one pier was leaning down river more than the other. Not surprisingly, the middle arch

had cracked diagonally under the strain, and the whole bridge was in a dangerous condition. So dangerous, in fact, that it was thought advisable to replace it with a temporary wooden bridge while the new stone one was built at a more leisurely speed. Lord Palmerston and neighbouring landowners signed an agreement for the waters to be stopped and diverted during building, and then, with work completed, Romsey could at last welcome travellers from the west with confidence and a clear conscience.

Middlebridge in the early 20th century
before being rebuilt with a lower arch in the 1930s

Romsey's Canal

A little later, in the 1790s, the Andover-Redbridge canal was constructed to the east of town after some century of discussion. The wharf at Romsey, at the present-day Plaza roundabout, was well placed along the canal's length. If the Southampton-Salisbury Canal had come to fruition, it would have looped through the Andover-Redbridge Canal at Romsey, which would have achieved considerable significance from its position. As it was, the canal had only a short life before the coming of the railways. The one notable advantage of the canal was the ease with which large amounts of cheap coal could be transported to the town, a benefit to the new local gas company in the 1830s.

The Expansion of Industry

Alongside its new-found service industry, the economic life of Romsey improved overall. Paper-making, having made a tentative early start at Rivermead Mill, now breathed new life into those of Romsey's other mills that could no longer make a living from fulling cloth. The preparation of paper pulp required similar pounding techniques to those of the medieval fulling-mills: so owners of redundant fulling-mills thankfully turned to paper-making. The mills became important employers with substantial numbers of workers, male and female. Some nine mill-sites have been identified for Romsey, mainly devoted to corn-milling and paper-making in the 18th century, many of them with several waterwheels per site. Flax-processing became a major milling activity by the early 1800s.

By that time, most of the mills had secondary activities within their bounds, including oil-skin dressing, timber-sawing and whiting works. Tanning continued, as it had for centuries, but now helped by the introduction of small waterwheels for grinding bark and driving pumps, together with other improvements for smoother production. Even the agricultural climate probably showed a short-term improvement, as all the local farms began to benefit from an unsettled Europe and the restrictions on imports during the Napoleonic wars.

The war years, however, were not kind to the poorer people as the 19th century dawned. Bread rose to an unprecedented price that would not be matched or exceeded until well into the 20th century. It accentuated the plight of those - particularly in rural Romsey - who had not been able to benefit from the economic revival of the late 1700s.

But their dismal outlook was not shared by those who rode on the wave of success associated with the coaching trade. Expectations rose. An embryonic sense of hygiene, and a new cultural fastidiousness, led to the appointment in the mid-1700s of a town scavenger to clean the streets. He was paid £10 a year, the money being raised by a 1½d levy on the inhabitants. Whether this official managed to deal with the irresponsible folk who left their dung-heaps along the road or the butchers who left their butchery-blocks in the way of passers-by is not certain.

Everyone's Health

Despite the careless attitude of some, health improved and more people lived longer. Dr Latham, checking the burial registers, was able to report triumphantly on the increasing number of inhabitants now reaching a great age. This success owed much to a positive attempt to control illness. The poor were included in the overall care of inhabitants, partly out of compassion but partly also out of a growing realisation that, if the poor were neglected, infections would remain endemic throughout society. Town hall accounts for 1742 reveal that Messrs Cowley and Blundell were paid 5s 0d for supplying medicines to the poor, and a midwife was paid 5s 0d.

More dramatically, in the second half of the 18th century, came the campaign against smallpox. Dr Henry O'Neill, several times mayor of Romsey, introduced Jenner's smallpox inoculation to the town. He used Jermyns House at Ampfield as his base and was instrumental in helping to alleviate the disease. Dr O'Neill's reputation did not help his son, also Henry, to recoup the costs he incurred in medical expenses for the poor. In 1784 the town hall accounts indicate that he was refused recompense of £8 8s 0d for treating the sick. It was stated that he had 'no orders to treat - Messrs Seward and Bartlett having undertaken the care of the poor'. The medical care of the poor was obviously tendered for in the same way as the running of the workhouse. In 1787, Seward and Bartlett were paid 20 guineas for inoculations for the poor. Dr Godwin Seward also built an isolation hospital at Woodley. Although there were still 13 recorded deaths from smallpox in Romsey during 1800, there had been a definite improvement in loss of life from this dreadful disease.

Generally, indeed, there was an increasing awareness, if not true understanding, of a need for basic sanitation, even though it would take a long time before all were persuaded of the advantages of cleanliness. There was also a move to wean the victims of gin-drinking from their health-destroying habits. Ale-houses were encouraged as more wholesome alternatives to the notorious gin-drinking; quite a few of Romsey's ale-houses originated in this way. Alongside the reduction in deaths by prophylactic methods, the number of inhabitants was also inflated by some 300 refugees from the French Revolution during the 1790s, and later by opponents to Napoleon.

New Building
Such growth promoted in turn much new building. As the townspeople thrived, so their increasing numbers brought prosperity to those involved in the building industry. Many Romsey houses, small as well as grand, can be dated to the end of the 18th and beginning of the 19th century. Existing properties were enhanced with modern brick facades. House insurances, a new fashion, hastened a change from thatched to tiled roofs - lower premiums were demanded for tiled roofs.

Within the town, a dynasty of brickmakers and bricklayers became very successful. The Floyds can be traced throughout the whole of the late Georgian period, almost every member, from Gabriel Floyd in 1740, being a bricklayer. Even the one exception, Henry Floyd, who became an innkeeper, kept a Banning Street pub called *The Bricklayers Arms*, which must have been largely patronised by members of his own family. So successful did the Floyds become that one of the numerous Thomas Floyds was able to leave to his wife and three daughters eight houses and other buildings that he owned, mostly in The Hundred and Banning Street. One Henry Floyd gained another sort of fame as the fattest man known.

Broadlands was in the vanguard of this building boom. The first Lord Palmerston had visually enhanced his home by altering the flow of the River Test to give a splendid sweep of water in front of the house. Now his successor almost completely rebuilt Broadlands, creating a Palladian mansion and landscaping the grounds with the help of the famed 'Capability' Brown. In this splendid setting, the second Lord Palmerston and his wife entertained luminaries such as the great artist Sir Joshua Reynolds, Count Rumbold (founder of the Royal Institution) and the playwright, Sheridan.

Education
Lady Palmerston also turned her attention to the education of girls in Romsey. In 1799, she founded a 'school of industry'. This school was dedicated to teaching girls basic literacy and, predominantly, needlework and housewifery skills. It was sited

in Church Street at an unestablished location, and opened with 31 girls. By 1803, when the numbers had doubled, a separate section had been set up for 'mixed' infants. In a single year Lady Palmerston spent £1,000 on this charity.

Little is known about female education before this time. There is just a brief reference to Sir William Petty's endowment paying 'Alice Stork for teaching 4 girls about 12 years old plain needlework for the space of 1 year at 10 shilling each'. Otherwise, it can only be assumed that some girls may have attended dame schools.

Indeed, there is very little information about any schooling until the end of the 18th century, but demands on education must have increased with population growth. Once again, the parish registers provide interesting information, particularly through marriage records. Although illegitimacy was rising, there seems also to have been a definite increase in the numbers getting married during the mid-1700s.

Over four years at the beginning of the 1700s the average number of marriages a year was just 13, but this figure had doubled by the 1740s, and increased further within another 20 years. In the year 1766, 32 couples were married - 20 of the grooms could sign the register, though rather fewer women. The rise in marriages probably reflects both a growing population and an improving economy that gave the more fortunate young people a secure basis for marriage.

The growth of industry and the new service occupations, together with the importance of sustaining links with the outside world, created a greater need for more people to have a basic education. Signatures, instead of 'marks', on documents do suggest a growing level of basic literacy, particularly amongst the men.

The beginnings of the Sunday schools offered opportunities that had never been so widely available before. The Congregational Church (United Reformed Church) set up its Sunday School in 1785 and the Abbey responded in 1792. One day a week, with much time obviously given to religious studies, was only a start, and could not provide a really sound basic education. At the beginning of the 19th century both the Anglican and Dissenting churches determined to broaden their ambitions for general education. They were to be encouraged in this by the promise of government grants.

By the early 1800s the third Lord Palmerston was complaining about the behaviour of a large number of boys who were being taught within the Abbey church. Their 'school' was conducted in the north-west corner of the nave, where a platform was inserted to create extra floor space. Records suggest there was also a school at the east end, though it is uncertain whether these operated at the same time and, if so, what relationship there was between the two.

The New Landless Poor: Agricultural Refugees
It is difficult to tell how much the surrounding rural area shared the opportunities opening up in the town. Just as Dr Latham reported differing views about work in urban Romsey, so there were similar mixed feelings about rural Romsey at the end of the 18th and beginning of the 19th centuries. The big landowners were encouraging inclosure, keen to amalgamate the smallest farms into larger units, which could then be leased for a longer term of years. This made for better investment in the land, and was supported in Parliament, where so many members had vested interest through their own estates. The final intensive inclosure activities in the Romsey area have left for posterity a set of fascinating maps dated 1809. The principal beneficiaries were Lord Palmerston and the Fleming family.

Great swathes of open land that had been held in common by several property holders of varying status were now carved up according to the degree of interest held. Each landowner then had to enclose his new holding. Although the ancient commons had never been public land, but land held in common by specific owners, many small tenants with ancient common rights were the losers, as their limited interest entitled them only to worthlessly small plots. Along with common rights, old established meandering ways across these open tracts were extinguished, and in their place appeared the wide straight interconnecting roads that are still identifiable as 'enclosure' roads.

With the final surge of inclosures in the early 1800s, the wealthier estate-holders around Romsey exchanged lands to consolidate their estates. They also began to organise their land into more efficient larger units for leasing out over longer terms of years. The tenants of these larger holdings prospered at the expense of the small tenant husbandman who, with his short-term lease, began to disappear. Over the following decades a new class of landless labourers emerged, later growing rapidly as a movement towards more pastoral farming meant that fewer farmworkers were needed. The dispossessed had to look elsewhere.

Many landless labourers were probably obliged to move into town centres. So far, though, there is no real link between the names of those who lost their holdings in rural Romsey and newcomers who joined the local urban throng. Maybe they found that the Romsey economy was already faltering, and could not absorb more unskilled people. Somehow they must have got work elsewhere, thus keeping clear of the settlement laws. Certainly, there is little evidence of them being returned from other parishes.

William Cobbett in his *Rural Rides* described the Romsey of 1826 in these words: 'This town was, in ancient times, a very grand place, though it is now nothing more than a decent market-town, without any thing to entitle it to particular notice, except the church ....'. As the era of the House of Hanover came to an end, so cracks appeared in the revived economy of Romsey. The boom years of the Napoleonic Wars faded, and several bankruptcies ruffled the confidence of the community. The economy had widened but it was not sustainable.

In this deteriorating situation, Romsey Infra and Romsey Extra each decided at last that it was time to purchase property to be used as a workhouse or poorhouse. Romsey Extra acquired a rather grand 18th-century house on the corner of Cupernham Lane, while Romsey Infra spent £678 on a house somewhere in Cherville Street, decreeing that the deeds of this Poorhouse be put in the parish chest. The town then ended the policy of 'farming' out care of the poor, and in November 1816 James Summers was appointed Superintendent of the Cherville Street Workhouse at a salary of ten shillings a week.

135

Effects of War: the Napoleonic aftermath

Towards the end of the Georgian era, attention was diverted to wider events, as first the French Revolution and then the Napoleonic Wars intruded on many aspects of life. The Napoleonic threat brought a real fear of invasion. Patriotism flourished in Romsey as elsewhere. The tangible evidence for this was realised in new enthusiasm for the local militia, the semi-voluntary, semi-conscripted home-guard of its day. Not everyone shared the patriotic feelings, though, and conscription was far from universally popular. All men under 40 years of age with fewer than four children were expected to register for the militia, offering justification for not being included in the ballot if they were unwilling. One hopeful, seeking exemption, claimed on his form that he suffered from 'the tooth'.

Waterloo Memorial
Romsey Abbey
south garth

The war years over, the bubble of the new trades began to burst. They were part of a wider, but also much more fragile economy. So much depended on the continued success of the coaching business and the need for water power. But even before livelihoods were put at risk by the advent of railways and the growth and spread of machine-driven processes, there was a downturn in individual fortunes. One of the major brewers went bankrupt in 1817 and a leading papermaker in 1830. Indeed, although the paper-mills went on until comparatively recently, no white paper was made anywhere in Romsey after the 1820s.

The brewer who went bankrupt was the son of Dr Latham, the local historian. It was a sad affair, resulting in Dr Latham's ruin as well as his son's, and the break-up of the bankrupt's Abbey Estate. This estate was the area west of the Abbey gateway, and is now largely occupied by a terrace of white-fronted houses. During the time of the brewery it must have been noisy and smelly with stable activities and brewing processes intermingling.

The town corporation bought the western part of his property (where Romsey Abbey church rooms now stand) and developed yet another town hall on the site in 1820, after which the now derelict Audit House was pulled down. The new town hall came just in time to welcome a broader-based corporation. The repeal, in 1828, of the 17th-century Test and Corporation Acts enabled followers of the dissenting faiths to enter civic affairs. The 'Latham' town hall was the first one in which they could exercise this right.

Romsey's third town hall
in use from 1820-1866

Romsey at the end of the Georgian period was a very mixed society. The landless labourer, who was the major loser in all the changes, eked out a miserable existence, often resorting to poaching, a widespread crime, which, in 1803, became a capital offence if capture was resisted. This led to the notorious case of Charles Smith, caught poaching on Lord Palmerston's Broadlands estate and hanged for wounding the game-keeper who tried to apprehend him. Although Lord Palmerston supported a petition for clemency, he was unpopular for some time.

At one level, then, life was unbelievably hard, but the upper echelon of Romsey society, though shadowed by the occasional fall of one of its members, was nevertheless enjoying a true 'never had it so good' feeling. Perhaps they were choosing not to look into the future. Their surroundings were improving. The Pavement Commission, set up in 1811, was gradually making the town a pleasanter place to move about - providing pavements, improving cleanliness, and introducing street lighting, first with oil lamps and later with gas. The more affluent people socialised together with dancing at assemblies and a life-style generally associated with Jane Austen. There was a feeling amongst the more fortunate that nothing need, should or would change.

Indications from the Trade Directories
The larger, more cosmopolitan population expected better communications, and Romsey Post Office developed with Moses Pepper as the postmaster. Mr Pepper's main business was a draper's shop in the Market Place (now the National Westminster Bank) and his role as postmaster was only a side-line, much as several other businessmen took on insurance agencies. Pigot's 1830 trade directory for Romsey states:

> 'Letters from London arrive, by mail-cart from Winchester, every morning at a quarter before seven, and are despatched by the same conveyance every evening at 8. Letters from Bristol arrive every morning at 3, and are despatched every evening at 11. Letters from Portsmouth and Southampton arrive every night at 11, and are despatched every morning at 3.'

The same 1830 trade directory describes the town's economy with a succinct - and rather disparaging - contemporary view of the town as the Georgian period ended:

> 'This town had formerly a considerable clothing trade; but that business has almost entirely disappeared, and the only vestige of it is the manufacture of a few shalloons. Employment is found by some persons here in the making of sackings; there are also paper works, tanneries and matting concerns.'

HATS AND CAPS.

M. PEPPER AND SON

Have received a large stock of Hats for the Spring Season, in all the newest shapes; also Felt and Straw Hats, and Cloth and Tweed Caps, in a great variety of shapes.

THE VICTORIAN AGE: An Economic See-Saw

Prelude: The Reign of William IV

The reign of William IV, sandwiched inconspicuously between those of George IV and Victoria, appears almost as a prelude to the Victorian age, but had a significance of its own. William's brief seven-year reign, from 1830 to 1837, stands out as the great time of Parliamentary reform with repercussions that affected all parts of the country, including Romsey. It was a watershed in the life-style of the nation.

Some of the reforming acts had little obvious direct effect on the inhabitants of Romsey. It is unlikely that more than a small minority were concerned about the 1832 Reform Bill that sought to redress the inadequacies and anomalies of representation in Parliament. Romsey had never had a borough member of Parliament, having always been represented by County MPs. Similarly, one of the early Factory Acts and the Abolition of Slavery, though undoubtedly a subject of earnest discussion among some citizens, would not have touched closely on day-to-day life in Romsey.

The 1833 Education Act, however, which initiated State grants to the two voluntary educational societies, had considerable effect. Lord Palmerston was inspired to lead a generous subscription list for a new boys' school, for which he gave the land. He had been appalled by the 'dilapidations' in the Abbey churchyard, caused by the boys who attended the school that was run within the north-west corner of the church itself. By 1835 Romsey, under the auspices of the Church of England, had its first Boys' National School at the bottom of Middlebridge Street; the St Barbe charity for boys was incorporated into this. The school was much needed, as there were 130 boys to be taught. The new building provided two rooms, a large one and a smaller one with a gallery. A convenient stream at the back of the property provided a good location for the privies.

The 1834 Poor Law Amendment Act also brought about a change in the way that the Romsey poor were served. Romsey Infra, Romsey Extra and some of the surrounding villages amalgamated their resources to form the Union of Workhouses where the Nightingale House complex now stands. The

139

authorities were aiming to comply with the new laws, which established locally elected Boards of Guardians of the Poor. Under the terms of the Act these guardians were expected to provide a harsh workhouse regime rather than outrelief, the idea being to make provisions unattractive to scroungers. So began the stringent Victorian practice of separating husbands, wives and children in the workhouse.

Fortunately, the system seems not to have been as badly abused in Romsey as elsewhere - there was certainly nothing to rival the Andover Workhouse Scandal. Nevertheless, the workhouse inhabitants became the great unwanted. In earlier centuries the poor had been accepted as a necessary problem - only the work-shy were resented. Now they were all shunted to the outskirts of town, much as the medieval lepers had been.

The Municipal Reform Act of 1835, closely following the repeal of the Test and Corporation Acts in 1828, opened up the field of local government still further. This 1835 Act ended the practice whereby councillors had nominated those they felt worthy of filling vacant seats on the council; henceforth all councillors were to be elected. Council matters consequently became of greater interest to those who were on the electoral roll, which was to be subject to a continually expanding franchise.

The election of councillors removed the final stranglehold of the 'old brigade' on the Council. Adherents of the dissenting churches were really able to participate in the civic life of their own community, and they injected new vigour into local affairs. Many businessmen, teachers and craftsmen, previously excluded by their religious beliefs, were finally entitled to contribute their skills to the full. The pattern of local government was enriched by this broader inclusion. The whole spectrum of the middle classes - at last a recognisable group - enjoyed local power, though still tending to leave national politics to the gentry.

Another Parliamentary act that had long-term significance was the Tithe Commutation Act of 1836. This was essentially a tidying-up procedure, whereby all tithes were commuted into monetary payments, and the values of such payments established. Many tithes had already been commuted, but this had occurred on an *ad hoc* basis over the centuries, and the Act consolidated the position. At the time, the Act only impinged on landholders, both owners and tenants, but the drawing of tithe maps and the recording of schedules have unintentionally provided historians with an indispensable record of land ownership and usage for the early Victorian period. It has also conserved the old field-names and the landlord-tenant relationships, as well as the complex situation concerning tithe-free and chargeable land, dating back to the time when tithes had originally been conceived as a contribution to the church.

Coincidentally, the church at this time lost its legal responsibility for registering births deaths and marriages as the 1836 Act for Registration centralised this function at Somerset House in London. Local civil register offices were set up.

More commercially, William IV's reign also saw the development of the use of gas both as a fuel and a means of lighting. Romsey's gas company began in 1833, the Andover-Redbridge canal delivering the necessary supply of cheap coal. Splendid gas lamps gave elegance and good lighting to the streets, and many leading citizens became shareholders.

But throughout the south of England, during this period, life was particularly grim in the farming community, where the effects of inclosure and other changes still hit hard. The 1795 'Speenhamland' system of calculating poor relief had also encouraged the depression of wages paid to farm labourers, reducing them and their families to a state of dangerous poverty. The resulting unrest won the sympathy of many educated people such as William Cobbett, but was viewed with distrust by the majority of landowners and the wider gentry.

The so-called 'Swing' Riots surfaced in 1830. They took their name from 'Captain Swing' - a fictitious writer of threatening letters to farmers, landowners and newspapers - and assumed a variety of forms. Some rioters attacked new-fangled farm machinery; others besieged local clergy demanding a reduction in tithe payments, or attacked the homes of wealthy members of the community. Tales of actions taken at Stockbridge and Andover, Southampton and the New Forest must have come to the ears of local inhabitants. On the southern edge of Romsey, there were disturbances at Luzborough. To the north, four Timsbury men were transported to Australia for damaging farm machinery at Michelmersh. It seems, however, that there were no Romsey men among the few Hampshire ringleaders to be hanged after the surge of unrest had ended. Nor is there any evidence that Romsey labourers, whether linked with agriculture or more urban industries, were involved in any union movements, unlike labourers elsewhere, who put their support behind unions rather than seeking enfranchisement.

The 1830s drew a line under many archaic practices, did much to stimulate new attitudes among and towards the deprived classes, and generally saw the introduction of a new way of life. In the year that William IV came to the throne, for example, the Liverpool to Manchester railway opened; in the year that he died the pillory was being used for the last time. The Victorian age was being well primed to have its own identity.

Victoria Regina

By the time that Victoria came to the throne in 1837, the national railway system was already spreading rapidly, but Romsey had to wait a further ten years before the first train came to the town, drawn by an engine named *Rhinoceros*. Many of the local gentry had been keen to encourage the new form of transport, but Romsey itself did not offer much attraction to the aspiring rail companies. When the London & South-Western Railway did at last create the Bishopstoke to Salisbury line through Romsey in 1847, the town was really only a stopping place en route to Salisbury. But, although the railway barely made contact with the town, some found year-round work there, and it was fortunate for the long-term prosperity of the town that it acquired a station at this early critical point in railway development.

The station was placed rather inconveniently beyond the edge of town as it then was, and for several decades the new form of transport was a mixed blessing for Romsey. It helped to keep the market buoyant, but had a highly detrimental effect on the coaching trade, and encouraged some people to leave the town.

During a period when some places, such as Birmingham, were booming and mushrooming to unbelievable sizes, taking the national population from 22 million to 38 million, Romsey stayed more or less static. This contrasts with an increase of about 1,000 inhabitants between 1800 and 1820.

Date	1821	1831	1841	1851	1861	1871	1881	1891
Number of Inhabitants	5,128	5,432	5,347	5,654	5,484	5,681	5,579	5,635

Population Figures for Romsey Infra and Romsey Extra (1821-1891 Censuses)

The Andover-Southampton rail link, built in the 1860s, was the final blow to the struggling coaching trade, which collapsed in the face of this new competition. As a result there was failure in other local businesses that were dependent on both long and short distance travellers coming into the heart of the town.

The canal had also ceased operation. It had, in fact, been bought out by the Andover-Southampton railway company whose original intention was to construct its rail link over the entire line of the canal. The stretch at Romsey survives as the result of a grand scheme promoted by Lord Palmerston to his advantage. Lord Palmerston was one of the few local people to benefit from the railway in its early years. He negotiated with the Andover-Southampton railway company, offering land to the east - where the railway runs today by Botley Road - in exchange for the Southampton Road being moved to run alongside the defunct canal south of the Plaza roundabout. The wall around Broadlands Park was also part of the deal, and Lord Palmerston's privacy was greatly enhanced.

Amongst other local people who advanced their position through the development of the railway was the Hon. Ralph Dutton of Timsbury Manor - for whom Duttons Road was not only named but made, to ease his journey home. He became a director of the London & South-Western Railway Company in 1854 and its chairman in 1875. There was also Sir Sam Fay who retired to his home at Awbridge Danes having risen up through the ranks to manage the Great Central Railway. Success at a less exalted level came to Thomas Hoof of Elm Close in Winchester Road (now replaced by a terrace of red-brick houses, built 2000). As a partner in the firm Hoof & Hill, he was a major railway contractor on the 1847 line from Bishopstoke to Salisbury.

The town generally, though, saw little to rejoice in once the novelty had worn off. Indeed, one poor man, a Mr Bundy was killed within months of the first railway opening. He was hit by the 10am train when trying to cross the railway line at Romsey, and was thus probably the first local railway fatality.

For a while Romsey stagnated. Some of the old canal employees found work on the railway, but on the whole there was little new work around to replace the trade that had been part of the turnpike system. It was a grim time for ordinary people. There had been general concern for the unemployed when William Lintott's flax-mill at the end of Abbey Water closed down in 1832 - a time when work had been suspended at several Romsey mills - but on that occasion it was revitalised by a new owner, Samuel Thompson. Even so it only lasted another twenty years or so as a flax-mill. In the 1860s it was converted into a corn-mill, which continued until it was burnt down in 1925. The paper-mills lost their way and the only really successful milling in the mid-19th century related to saw-milling, which thrived whilst the railways were being built, by supplying sleepers for the track and other vital needs. Corn-grinding remained successful at Town Mill as well as Abbey Mill, but did not require as large a work-force as the other milling processes that had failed.

It was in this context that another dissenting group, the Methodists, established themselves in Romsey during the early 19th century. The Wesleyans bought a chapel in Banning Street in 1813 with the breakaway Primitive Methodists building a separate chapel in The Hundred, near the Alma Road junction, in 1845. Later, each built anew, passing one another in their respective moves - the Wesleyans to a soaring new building in The Hundred and the Primitive Methodists to Middlebridge Street. During the century, Anglican chapels-of-ease were also built in Romsey Extra at Ridge, Lee and Crampmoor.

The fortunately affluent inhabitants of Victorian Romsey, like their counterparts elsewhere, felt that their responsibility lay in supporting grand community projects rather than subsidising the Poor Law. So money was found for these new churches, and for similar undertakings, such as schools.

In 1842, the new streamlined farming community established the Romsey Agricultural Society, which initially held its shows within the town itself. It was essentially a Christmas fat stock sale, and afterwards there was a 'men-only' celebratory dinner: in 1859 up to 90 sat down for this meal. The show was spread around the town centre with pigs in the Pig Market (now the Cornmarket), cattle and sheep on the Abbey green and horticultural stalls in the Market Place (and, after they had been built, in the Corn Exchange and the present town hall).

These efforts may have helped the fairs, which seem to have been successful during the mid-19th century. The Easter Fair of 1848 featured cheeses and livestock. Animals spilled over from the Market Place, lining the length of The Hundred as far as the police station and along Church Street to the Horsefair. Cheeses arrived by waggon from as far afield as Somerset and Dorset. Some 200 tons of cheese were sold at one fair.

Despite these successes, the narrowing of the agricultural focus in rural Romsey dragged the town further into economic stagnation. The middle of the 19th century was also dogged by frightening illnesses.   A widespread cholera epidemic, the scourge of the Victorian era and ferocious enough to worry central government, directly affected Romsey.   John Denner Blake, Romsey shoemaker, recorded in his 1848 journal the deaths from cholera of some twelve of his fellow inhabitants, noting also the death of a child from smallpox. He was relieved when the cholera epidemic was waning sufficiently for a thanksgiving service to be held.

This spell of debilitating illness, followed some decades later by the national agricultural depression of the late-19th century, for a while even counter-balanced the improvements brought about by the promising growth in the urban-based brewing industry and one or two other later 19th-century businesses.

Romsey and the Crimean War
Two major wars punctuated the Victorian era - the Crimean War in the 1850s and the Boer War that began as Victoria's reign ended. Romsey sent soldiers to both, and so had cause to celebrate their ends. The Crimean War was probably closer to the hearts and minds of the townspeople, though, because

Lord Palmerston of Broadlands was so closely involved as Prime Minister. The town was proud of 'Good Old Pam'. And just outside Romsey at Embley Park in Wellow, lived the great heroine of the Crimean War, Florence Nightingale. Peace celebrations were all the greater because of these links.

Local Administration and Official Buildings
Meanwhile, whatever was happening in the wider world, the corporation was busy responding to the various government acts relating to such local concerns as care of the poor, health and education. Subsequent to the 1834 Poor Law Amendment Act, there were, for example, a Public Health Act in 1848 in the wake of the cholera panic, the Burials Act of 1853 and the 1870 Education Act. Due to the good work of the local church societies, Romsey was already well provided for educationally; so there was no need to set up a School Board to introduce and supervise an educational system in the town. The Abbey churchyard, though, was desperately overcrowded and constituted a health hazard.

A Burial Board was set up. It was responsible for the new cemetery that opened in Botley Road in 1857 - an essential provision as the overflowing Abbey churchyard no longer complied with new regulations about depth of burial. Two cemetery chapels were built at Botley Road, one Church of England and the other Nonconformist, a pleasing reflection of the more open membership of the Council. Both chapels were designed by London architect, Robert Lower, son of a Romsey businessman. The Burial Board records contain a rather anxious letter from a prospective keeper, hoping to live in the cottage at the cemetery gates. He promised that his children would not clamber over the cemetery walls.

And, despite the sluggish economy, Romsey followed the example of other market towns by having a spurt of grand building in the 1860s. To the chagrin of the Corporation, the Corn Exchange came first, in 1864, originally with tall arched windows that set the tone for the style of yet another town hall. The latter opened in 1866, just too late for Lord Palmerston to enjoy. More modestly, the police station with its facade of dressed flint had already appeared in The Hundred in the 1840s.

A slightly more sophisticated fire service was provided in the 19th century. There appear to have been two fire engines during that period. The older of the two, was hand drawn, but the other could be horse-drawn. As the horses were hired from a local hostelry, and not always immediately available, the fire service must have been a very uncertain affair. Curiously, one of the engines was stored in the north apse of Romsey Abbey, presumably because the stone walls of the Abbey were considered protective. The other was kept behind double doors in Church Street at the Market Place end of Ashley Terrace.

Other groups besides the local authorities were responsible for impressive public buildings that were built or rebuilt during the 19th century. In 1855 the foundations were laid for Romsey's first purpose-built vicarage (now a private house known as Folly House, taking its name from the medieval window frames, placed in the garden by the Rev. E.L. Berthon during restoration of the north wall of the Abbey nave).

The Present Town Hall

It was during the 1880s that the Wesleyan Methodists and the Congregationalists acquired their new buildings - with ancillary accommodation as well as the church itself; and La Sagesse Convent soon followed on the rear part of the Abbey Mill site beyond the end of Abbey Water. The arrival of the sisters of La Sagesse, a French order founded by St Louis de Montfort, marked the return of an official Roman Catholic presence in the town.

Education
New schools also became a feature of the townscape. Like the 1835 Boys' National School in Middlebridge Street, they punctuated the edge of town as it then was, utilising cheaper land and illustrating the maxim that children should be seen but not heard. Like the unfortunates in the workhouse, Victorian schoolchildren were relegated to the fringes of Romsey's life.

147

The aim was to provide purpose-built schools jointly financed by state grants and church societies. The 46 girls listed at the Romsey National Day School in 1846 had to wait a little longer than their male counterparts. Their Church Lane school was only opened in 1851, and Lady Palmerston's School of Industry was absorbed as a special class within this new school, which also catered for mixed infants. It is now Romsey Abbey Primary School, and the oldest school building in the town still being used for its original purpose. Its opening also prompted the development of Church Lane as a through road.

While the 'National' girls were waiting for their own building, a charity school was erected in Middlebridge Street. In the 1840s the Nowes Charity had sufficient income to commission a new school for its boys, many of whom went on to successful apprenticeships also sponsored by the charity. The Nowes Charity School cost about £700 and, like the police station, was given an impressive facade of dressed flint. The revenue for the Nowes Charity unfortunately diminished swiftly during the late 19th century, and the building became a private house.

Extending their Sunday School work, the Nonconformists supported full-time education through their representative body, The British and Foreign Bible Society. Their Romsey school in The Hundred - usually known simply as The British School - opened in 1847. It was erected 'for the children of the poor without distinction of religious denomination'. Boys were in one section and girls and mixed infants in another, each with a separate entrance. With a facade reputedly designed by Florence Nightingale's father and her sister, Parthenope, it has since been converted into private dwellings facing up Alma Road and named English Court.

In the 1850s, Congregationalists attending evening service complained of the unbearable stuffiness after successive Sunday school classes had filled their church. So members financed a suite of sturdy brick buildings to the west of their church. It provided classrooms for hundreds of children each week. Indeed, all the Sunday Schools remained popular and well attended. Their 'treats' were definite highlights, when children paraded in their best clothes, usually processing to Broadlands Park to enjoy games and a picnic. Quite often

148

children simply attended the church, Sunday school and day school nearest their home. They changed schools occasionally, when there was trouble or parents fell behind with payments.

After the 1870 Education Act had made elementary schooling compulsory - though not free until 1891 - the pressure on the Boys' National School in Middlebridge Street increased. A new building was considered necessary. So, in 1872, the 'National' boys moved to a new school in Station Road (now the Public Library). The land was given by the Fleming family and the splendid modern building was designed by William Nesfield, a well-known architect. He was commissioned by the Rt Hon. William Cowper-Temple of Broadlands who had largely funded the project, and who is the unnamed 'parishioner' acknowledged in the stone plaque to the right of the entrance.

Pressure of space also caused problems at the British School but in this case they were solved by an extension added in the 1890s. This supplemented an earlier addition, a separate boys' school at the rear of the original school. With further space being taken up by a block of eternally troublesome toilets, there was very little playground left for the children. Fortunately, the ecumenical philosophy of William Cowper-Temple prevailed, and he made a playing field available in Alma Road.

Private schools and academies were the exception to the rule of dedicated buildings. There were many private schools in Romsey, providing for both day and boarding pupils. Indeed, the mid- to late-19th century was the hey-day for these establishments. Their owners generally leased large houses such as Wykeham House in The Hundred or Cherville House on the corner of Mill Lane and Church Road. The majority lasted only a few years, but a couple thrived for several decades in imposing 18th-century buildings.

Osborne House School was established in Church Street during the 1850s by John Frederick Osborne and his wife. At first it took boys and girls but, after Mrs Osborne's health failed, it became a boys' school only. The school was well-regarded and Mr Osborne became a respected member of Romsey society. He was mayor in 1877 and 1885.

Mrs Withers started her school at Bickleigh House in the Cornmarket (lying back to the right of the cutway through to the bus station), but in the early 1850s, with three children of her own under the age of five, she determinedly moved to much grander premises in Harrage House. Hers was one of the few schools catering for girls.

The South of England Educational Home for Young Ladies
Harrage House, The Hundred
By kind permission of Miss Betty Burnett

For some 25 years she offered a sophisticated education for select young ladies. By 1871 she had 50 girl boarders, many coming from the far-flung parts of the Empire where their parents were stationed. Four resident governesses and a 'Parisienne' helped her deliver a wide curriculum stretching to Foreign Languages, Botany, Geology and Architecture. Lord Palmerston bought Harrage House in 1859, and during his lifetime Mrs Withers wrote him overwhelmingly effusive letters. Indeed, rumours in town spoke of their close relationship. By 1880 Mrs Withers had left Romsey; Mr Withers had departed much earlier.

In 1887 the Misses Phillips started another girls' boarding school in the same Bickleigh House that had seen the start of Mrs Withers' educational enterprise. This new school continued well into the next century.

One rather special Romsey school was established in 1891 by the Bishop of Portsmouth. It was an orphanage and school for parentless Catholic boys from all over Hampshire, and the Bishop invited the grey-robed Sisters of La Sagesse to run this school in their Convent behind Abbey Mill. It was called St Joseph's Orphanage.

The Union Workhouse also had its own internal school for a while. Later, though, the Workhouse children were sent to the nearest school, which was the British School.

Poor Law Administration

In 1837 Josiah George, pillar of the Baptist Chapel, noted compassionately that a family of parents and five children was struggling on a total income of 11s 0d a week, the father earning 9s 0d and his eldest son, aged 14 years, bringing in a further 2s 0d. Their weekly rent was 2s 0d, and they had hardly any garden to help make them self-reliant. It would cost the authorities no less than 18s 0d a week, on very frugal terms, to maintain such a family of seven in the workhouse.

The outlook was bleak. The changes envisaged by the 1835 Poor Act did not happen overnight. Although complying with the Act by appointing Guardians yearly, the first in 1835, the administration continued to be recorded in the Vestry books, and Overseers were also still appointed. The Poor Law Commission instructed the Vestry to continue with their rate assessments 'pro tem', and the first meeting of the new Romsey Union was not held until 1851.

Around 1837, however, Romsey Infra Parish had sold their old Cherville Street poor house - a converted malthouse - for over £900. Freehold premises in Newton Lane, used to house paupers, were also sold. It seems the poor were by this time all being sent to the Union Workhouse. *The Hampshire Independent* of 13th September 1851 said:

It is a notable fact that the Union Workhouse has now a less number of inmates than can ever be remembered. Out of a Union population of nearly 11,000 the house [workhouse] contains but 64 paupers. This satisfactory state of things must however be attributed to a very large degree to its judicious discipline and management.

In view of this last daunting statement it is not surprising that many tried to avoid resorting to the workhouse.

Romsey Extra parish agreed in 1840 to give up to £100 to help five specially selected poor families to emigrate to Australia. Similarly in 1849 a 15 year old Wellow lad in the Union workhouse was given £10 by his parish for his proposed emigration 'due provision to be made for his comfort on the voyage and also when he landed in Australia'. Frustratingly, nothing more is heard of any of them.

Romsey Abbey

Those who left must have carried an enduring image of Romsey dominated as ever by its Abbey. Although close inspection showed the church to be poorly maintained and even ill-used, little disturbed the outward tranquillity of that great Norman building. It remained a constant, seemingly unchanging, part of the townscape. At some time it had acquired a square black clock, to be replaced towards the end of the century with another square clock, this time with a white dial. Although there were other adjustments to the exterior, it looked overall very much as it had ever done.

Inside, though, more obvious changes were happening. Since the early 17th century at least, its interior walls had been regularly whitewashed, a recognised means of preserving stonework which also tallied well with the growing Puritan preference for simplicity. The vibrant picture-stories of the medieval church were covered over, and the outlines of carvings blurred under countless applications of whitewash, applied regularly by men in receipt of poor relief. The effect was said to resemble the inside of a great chalk-pit. Over time, seating galleries had been added close to the crossing, and archways had been blocked in a vain attempt to keep out draughts. The whole building was cold, damp and cluttered with ill-kept pews.

The internal accretions were gradually removed under the direction of two 19th-century vicars, the Hon. Gerard Noel in the 1830s and the Rev. E.L. Berthon throughout his long ministry from 1860 to 1892. The Rev. Berthon had a specific skill to offer: he was an imaginative design engineer.

Over the 32 years of his ministry, he put his skills to good use in the Abbey. He reset the east windows and re-roofed the north transept. He found and renovated a medieval screen, replaced two windows in the north wall of the nave, and oversaw the relocation of the 1858 Walker organ. Perhaps his most appreciated work was the introduction of Gurney stoves in a valiant attempt to warm the building for long-suffering worshippers; in this he was supported by Lord Palmerston who died five years after Berthon's arrival.

Broadlands and the Prime Minister

Lord Palmerston's statue gazed down upon the affairs of the Market Place from shortly after his death in 1865. The town had always taken a vicarious pride in being the country residence of the famous Prime Minister, and his arrivals at Romsey railway station on his way back to Broadlands from his London home were always greeted with bells or, later, a gun salute. During his life-time he was held in deep respect, despite a wave of revulsion over the Charles Smith affair; he was popularly known as 'Good Old Pam'. Lord Palmerston took enormous interest in all aspects of the town, continuing to support his mother's school of industry, and giving to both the Abbey and the nonconformist chapels. He was closely involved with plans for the present town hall, though sadly he died before its completion. He was fastidious about personal hygiene, and concerned himself particularly with the health and cleanliness of the town, firing off letters to the Corporation, urging them to take action to avoid the dreaded typhus and cholera epidemics. He was well justified.

Broadlands after Palmerston

Lord and Lady Palmerston married late in life, some two years after the death of her first husband, Lord Cowper. Broadlands subsequently passed to her younger son, William Cowper, who then added on the Palmerston family name, Temple, to become the Rt Hon. William Cowper-Temple.

The Descent of Broadlands
since its purchase by the first Lord Palmerston in 1736

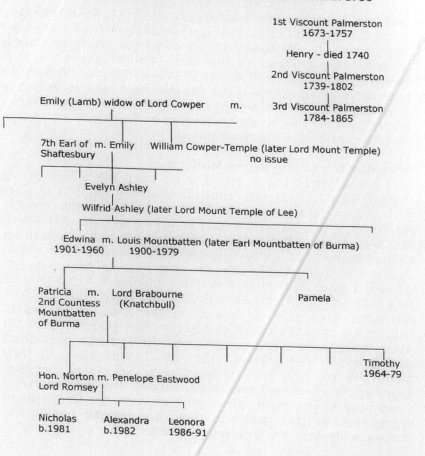

1st Viscount Palmerston
1673-1757

Henry - died 1740

2nd Viscount Palmerston
1739-1802

Emily (Lamb) widow of Lord Cowper   m.   3rd Viscount Palmerston
1784-1865

7th Earl of m. Emily   William Cowper-Temple (later Lord Mount Temple)
Shaftesbury   no issue

Evelyn Ashley

Wilfrid Ashley (later Lord Mount Temple of Lee)

Edwina m. Louis Mountbatten (later Earl Mountbatten of Burma)
1901-1960   1900-1979

Patricia   m.   Lord Brabourne   Pamela
2nd Countess   (Knatchbull)
Mountbatten
of Burma

Timothy
1964-79

Hon. Norton m. Penelope Eastwood
Lord Romsey |

Nicholas   Alexandra   Leonora
b.1981   b.1982   1986-91

The first Lord Palmerston bought the Broadlands estate from Sir Humphrey Sydenham, heir of the St Barbe family, who had held the property since the late 16th century.

154

grants made for houses built by private builders in 1926 and 1927. Among these were four pairs of semi-detached houses built by Strong's Brewery in Duttons Road.

The Romsey Official Town Guide of 1936 contained the following information under the title 'Housing'.

'During the last few years a definite and successful start has been made to provide comfortable and up-to-date houses in the Borough for the working class at reasonable rents. Three separate Corporation Housing Schemes have been carried through, the last of which provided 68 houses, to give accommodation for families displaced from non-repairable or overcrowded houses in the congested areas. Since the enlargement of the Borough in 1932 many houses have been and are still being added to the town by private enterprise.'

This report does not wholly agree with the findings of the Council's Highways and Sanitary Committee, responsible for the state of existing housing in the borough from 1936. In the years between 1936 and 1940 there were numerous notices sent to landlords demanding demolition of properties in many parts of the centre of the town. Occasionally renovation work was allowed, but demand for demolition was more usual. The popular national term was 'slum clearance'.

Council house development continued on the immediate north of the town - Malmesbury Road, Duttons Road, Princes Road, and Jubilee Road were developed. People were moved to the new houses from the small overcrowded cottages in Latimer Street, Love Lane and similar streets. These 'congested areas' also included Church Court, adjacent to *King John's House*, where it was agreed that the owner needed to repair Nos 11, 13, 15, 17, 19, 21, 23 and 25: if Nos 2, 4 and 6 were not used for human habitation they need not be demolished.

In the event Nos 2, 4 and 6 Church Court were the subject of an exciting discovery in 1927. To quote Mr W.J. Andrew who wrote the first guide book to King John's House:

'In 1927 I was fortunate enough to be its discoverer. Until then its identity had remained unsuspected, for a projecting Tudor chimney stack, Georgian brick

193

doorways, and a coat of plaster over the whole, had suggested nothing more than a row of two or three old cottages.'

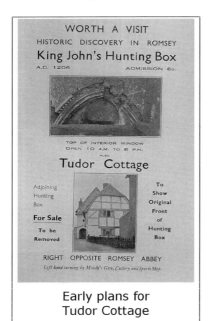

Early plans for Tudor Cottage

Walter Andrew, quite correctly, identified the main stone-built house as a 13th-century building. Research revealed that King John had built a hunting lodge in Romsey around 1206, and Mr Andrew was convinced that he had found this very place - hence the name, which has erroneously associated the property with King John ever since. Unfortunately, Walter Andrew was a little hasty in his deductions, and later evidence strongly suggests a building date of the mid-1250s, some forty years after King John's death. Miss Moody, the owner, opened a teashop in *Tudor Cottage*, and allowed visitors into King John's House.

The more affluent people continued the trend of moving up the hill on Winchester Road and into Cupernham. They were attracted by the generous space for larger houses and the healthier atmosphere above central Romsey's uncertain drainage arrangements.

Some existing large houses were sold and their land developed, just as part of Harrage Park had earlier been divided into several plots and The Crescent carved out of the old Mile Hill Estate. Smaller houses were built along Botley Road adjacent to the railway and in Winchester Road. Alma Road, Lord Palmerston's route from the railway station to Broadlands, ceased to be a road through fields. These developments were mainly the work of small builders who each built and sold a few houses - unlike the large-scale property companies of the late

20th century. This accounts for the changing style of terraces within a street, often reflecting old field boundaries as individual builders bought separate 'lots' at auction.

The housing of the poorer folk was continually the subject of comment by the Medical Officer of Health, and his annual reports contained much the same phrases for the first thirty years of the century:

> 'The general standard of housing in the town is poor - very poor for a country town. The houses are small, dark, ill-ventilated, set low on the ground, and (which is perhaps well) are without indoor sanitation or drains. ..... where they are in fair repair .... they make serviceable dwellings for poor people at the rentals at which they are obtainable.'

The minutes of the Highways and Sanitary Committee of the Romsey Corporation for 8th October 1936 include under the heading 'Housing Acts':

> Banning Street 29 & 29a - builder asked if he could reconstruct cottages rather than demolish them - refused.
>
> 15-24 Banning Street and 114-122 The Hundred - owner to demolish without delay - otherwise Council will do same and charge him.
>
> 10-20 Love Lane, 1-11 Barling Square - owner to be asked to demolish forthwith.
>
> Crown Court - closing orders to be made and tenants removed into Council Houses.
>
> 7-9 Latimer Street specified work had not been done - demolition order to be served.

One side effect of all the rebuilding within central Romsey was confusion for the postal service. To compensate, several streets had to be renumbered, occasionally more than once. An even more drastic amendment was made to the once rural reaches of northern Cherville Street. So much new building was springing up that it was decided to redesignate the upper section as Greatbridge Road.

All these new and renovated houses needed lighting, heating and cooking facilities. In the 1920s the gas company, as well as increasing its gas customers, considered supplying the town with electricity. Plans were drawn up for a generating station, but nothing came of the idea. The public electricity supply eventually arrived in Romsey in 1928, with Southampton Corporation providing bulk supply as far as its boundary. Beyond this point, the network was developed by the West Hampshire Electricity Company. However, electricity was not universally available until some twenty years later.

Roads
Street lighting, still only in the main part of the town, certainly continued to be by gas until the middle of the 20th century. Many street lights were hung from wall brackets, but there were also some lamp standards. These were often right on the edge of pavements or in the gutters, positions that would be disastrous today. Street direction signs were also often in positions that later became hazardous.

With the increase of wheeled traffic, urgent attention had to be given to the state of the road surfaces, and the first improvement was to spray bitumen until finally the present day tarmacadam surfaces were introduced. There is a note in the Romsey Town Council minutes of 1924 saying that bitumen spraying on main and secondary roads had been completed. In the same year the old water carts were sold off.

Speed was becoming an issue. In 1923 four drivers were fined £5 each for 'driving heavy motor cars at speeds exceeding 12 mph'. Their charabancs [coaches] had been timed over a measured distance of 440 yards at rates of up to 23mph.

The demolition of the Remount Camp may have triggered the straightening of the road from the top of Pauncefoot Hill so that it no longer took a dog-leg around Ranvilles Farm. Perhaps this had the worrying effect of encouraging faster speeds.

By 1929 traffic in the town centre was becoming a major problem, and the Town Clerk was asked to talk to the County Surveyor 'about a Bypass road' to run between the town and the northern edge of Broadlands Park. The new road was agreed and various buildings were demolished. The tenants of cottages south of the Tadburn stream were rehoused in Mill

196

Lane, where the County Council built new houses. Bartlett's Almshouses were replaced by new buildings in The Meads, designed by local architect, William Comely Roles. The Bypass and the re-fashioned Middlebridge were opened in 1931.

'On the Road'

There were others using the roads as well as the new car-owning fraternity. Between the First and Second World Wars, many unemployed travelled on foot from workhouse to workhouse, crossing the country to seek work. They stopped overnight in workhouse casual wards, called 'The Spike'. One week, in February 1931, saw 124 such desolate people in Romsey. It was reported that it was pitiful to see women, some with children, among those crowded into the cheerless ward, but many locals resented having to care for these 'visitors'. They felt they were bearing enough of a burden in supporting the one in four working class families 'on the dole' in Romsey. In the last week of September 1939 the average intake into the casual wards was 15 a night, but the advent of war changed all that. As men were conscripted into the armed services, unemployment virtually disappeared; the casual wards were to be kept available for possible civilian casualties.

Commerce and Industry

Shops were still scattered throughout the town, often small 'front room' businesses in streets such as Mill Lane, Banning Street and Winchester Road. In the centre there was a change of emphasis as national retailers moved in and it appears that, by 1923, The Hundred had taken much of the trade from Bell Street.

The general ambience of shopping, however, remained much the same. All goods remained behind the counter, to be shown by the assistant at the customer's request. In some shops, such as Guard's clothes departments, there were chairs for the customers, and all shops had errand boys to deliver goods to the house later in the day. There must have been a flurry of excitement in the 1930s, when artificial silk stockings came in as a glamorous alternative to wool or cotton.

Everything was done at a more leisurely pace, and the time taken in grocery shopping would be quite irksome in today's rush and hurry life-style. Coffee was roasted and ground, and gave off a wonderful aroma. Goods were kept in an assortment of containers - barrels and jute sacks for some commodities; 'tea' chests or large canisters for tea with other canisters for coffee beans; wooden boxes fixed to the wall for small items like caraway seeds and peppercorns. Butter and margarine were displayed on wooden slabs and served by being cut with butter pats, which were juggled to get the required quantity and shape - a fascinating procedure. Biscuits were displayed in tins supported and fixed along the front of the counter from which customers indicated their choice. Goods were then weighed on brass or iron weighing scales.

These grocery shops had a fascinating range of packing techniques. The common method in the 1920s and 1930s was to make a cone of thick blue paper and then, with a scoop, fill it with dry goods like rice, sugar, tea or beans. Butter and other fats, having been dragooned into shape, were crisply folded in crackling greaseproof paper.

The style of some shops changed. Chemists, for example, began to expand their lines of stock in the 1930s. Old-fashioned Romsey chemists, such as William Dodridge at 2 Church Street and Frank Oram at 4 Market Place, belonged to the era when a chemist was a pharmacist and perhaps a photographic dealer, but little else. Then Boots the Chemist, as it was known, extended its lines to associated goods and beyond, and others followed suit.

Kersey's the jewellers started as watch and clock makers in Romsey at the end of the 19th century. They were first in Bell Street and in 1903 moved to 3 The Hundred. The family continued to run their traditional shop, and also made a notable contribution to the local community by helping Smiths of Derby to erect the clock in the Abbey in 1924, a link that was to be maintained through the generations.

As the century progressed, some old established businesses moved with the times. Thomas Ely and Sons, ironmongers, whitesmiths and plumbers, developed their trade to include electrical work and the wireless (radio). An extract from *The*

Romsey Advertiser of 6th July 1923 concerns an early wireless concert:

> On Sunday evening Messrs Ely, Market Place, Romsey, who have a wireless apparatus attached to the roof of their premises, gave another concert. They have a loudspeaker placed in the first storey window from which the concert that is held at Marconi House, London, is heard. A large number of people assembled, who greatly appreciate Messrs Ely's courtesy to the public, many hearing the wonders of the wireless for the first time. After the traffic had stopped, each item was heard most distinctly. This is the fourth Sunday evening that these concerts have been heard.

Fresh food businesses, though, still had to follow traditional ways of keeping their food from deteriorating. In winter, Romsey fish shops and butchers had ice brought from Embley ice-house by wagon: Harding's, in the Market Place, used an old ice house as a store so that ice lasted until early summer. At summer weekends during the thirties, enterprising ice-cream manufacturers sent out salesmen on specially adapted tricycles with large boxes attached. These contained cartons of ice-cream, and the cycling salesmen rode round the streets ringing their bells to attract people's attention. There was a well-known advertising slogan, 'Stop me and buy one'.

The general slump throughout the country which set in at the beginning of the 1930s caused many shops to close. Perhaps surprisingly, the only Romsey shops that appear to have increased in number at that time were hairdressers and tailors, while newsagents and boot and shoe repairers also managed to keep their trade going.

Amongst the more industrial businesses, some, like the Berthon Boat Works, had disappeared from the scene after the 1914-18 war. The business of Cooper's, the milling engineers, closed after the slump in the early thirties, a sad end for a company that had made a valiant contribution to the First World War.

Others, however, managed to continue successfully, and to weather the storm of the depression in the 1930s. One such was Mitchell's Garage with its light engineering works. Its war work over, the business was growing in 1919, and moved from Fox Mill to Middlebridge Street - still then the main road to the west. It was the last petrol station before Lyndhurst and, before alterations, the sharp bends around Ranvilles Farm at the top of Pauncefoot Hill often caused difficulties for motorists, who then required assistance from Mitchell's.

Mitchell's also ran a car hire service and garaged the Romsey ambulance - providing a driver for it, when necessary. Petrol was still sold by the can - from shops in the town as well as from the 'motor engineers' such as Mitchell's, Rolfe's on Winchester Hill, and Wrynam's at the junction of Botley Road and Winchester Road. Out of town petrol stations, to serve the motorist travelling between distant towns, were first established by the Automobile Association in the 1920s.

On Winchester Hill Mr B.A. Rolfe developed 'Country Life Caravans', running in conjunction with the garage and petrol station, which had been opened in 1911. After making horse-drawn caravans for a short time, he then developed models to be towed by car. Caravans were not only built for leisure but were made to order for special projects, particularly for travelling medical and dental surgeries.

Wills Nursery - the 'Tomato Factory' - was a newcomer to the town in this period, and quickly became another important employer from its inception in 1926. Arthur Reynolds Wills came from the Lea Valley in Hertfordshire, where he had been apprenticed to a large-scale glasshouse business. After the War, when he decided to start up on his own, he recognised the need for a move to a cleaner area.

He eventually identified an ideal site on the flat land alongside the railway in Botley Road, Romsey. He met with the then owner, Lord Mount Temple (Col. Wilfrid Ashley), and in 1925 he managed with difficulty to purchase the 29 acres of land. At that time he recognised the need for careful planning of the site in the context of the adjacent railway and also the distant future potential of the site for housing.

Construction on the Botley Road site commenced in 1926, and Mr Wills soon had a railway siding installed to meet the expanding need for bulk supplies of fuel for the boilers and (initially at least) the dispatch of produce.

At that time unemployment in the town was high, and, having made contact with Mr Hughes at the Labour Exchange in Bell Street (adjacent to Leach's the drapers, now Smith Bradbeer's), Mr Wills surprised everyone by saying that he wanted to employ as many men and women as possible. He had been inspired by some of the business principles of Henry Ford I - particularly those relating to employees and banks. He believed that labour, if well managed, was the cheapest expense you could have, and that it was better not to be over reliant on banks and loans but rather to finance your business out of your own workshop by developing the skills of employees. It was best to make what you needed wherever practicable in preference to buying it - 'insourcing' as opposed to 'outsourcing' in the modern jargon.

The application of these principles enabled him to overcome the dilemma posed by a highly seasonal production workload that peaked in the growing season on the one hand, and the risks associated with having to recruit and train new employees each season in an unpredictable labour market on the other. He maintained continuity of employment and income for his workers throughout the year. There was no demarcation in the business, and this at a time when major industries were often brought to a standstill by 'who does what' disputes. By being with the employees every day and treating them as individuals he earned their confidence and made them keen to become multi-skilled.

In the face of the severe depression in 1929 and the need to remain solvent, the business was compelled to sell stocks of timber, and to raise some capital by building 24 houses in Tadburn Road for sale and rent. This speculative though temporary diversification saved the business from bankruptcy.

Strong's Brewery
The development of Strong's Brewery was such an important part of Romsey's history that it eventually overshadowed the other local industries. The policy of acquiring other breweries continued to widen the market. Travellers over the south and

west of England became familiar with signs proclaiming 'You are in the Strong country'. Over the main Horsefair gateway into the brewery there was an arch inscribed with the proud message 'The Heart of the Strong Country'. In the 1920s and the following decades, new buildings added dramatic features to the skyline with tower blocks and tall chimneys.

The company was one of the main employers of the town for the greater part of the 20th century. It encompassed many trades other than those directly involved in the brewing processes. In the early days, the produce was delivered by horse and wagon, later by steam wagon, and then by lorry, all forms of transport requiring different forms of maintenance. In the days of the horse drawn dray, part of the site was a paddock for the horses. The company was a self-contained business running its own coopers' shop, engineers' shop, motor repair shop and sign-writing shop. Before the Second World War there was already a large A & R (alteration and repair) Department for brewery work and for building and refurbishing public houses.

By 1930 the Brewery had been much enlarged with new buildings and new plant. Most employees worked from 6am to 5pm with half an hour for breakfast and one hour for dinner. The wages were similar to local agricultural pay - and skilled craftsmen had to serve a long apprenticeship with only token pay. There was overtime pay for Easter, Whitsun and prior to Christmas, and a Company profit-sharing scheme.

As with many other businesses, there was no sick pay and no company pension scheme, although long service employees were given an ex gratia payment of ten shilling per week - about a quarter of their weekly wage. There was no accident compensation scheme, but employees badly injured in accidents at work would usually be retained working at light tasks whenever possible. 'Walter Broomfield, partially crippled by the kick of a horse, chopped kindling wood when he felt inclined.'

There was one week's holiday with pay, an allowance of one quart of beer per day per person, free, and an annual day-outing - very often on a chartered train which carried the essential refreshment as well as the workers. The old daily beer allowance of half a gallon had been halved to one quart after a steam vehicle driver knocked down a wall whilst delivering beer in Bournemouth, and promptly claimed that his condition 'under the influence' was only due to his having consumed his daily allowance.

The distinctive roof-scape of Strong's Horsefair Brewery

The 1930s saw the change in the method of effluent disposal from the Brewery with the introduction of the sewage treatment works at Green Hill. Prior to this, the yeast sludge, ullage beer, caustic and other detergents from the brewery were all discharged into the Holbrook stream where it carried its stale beer-smelling frothy brown liquid to the river Test, in company with the contents of domestic privies also situated on the banks of the same stream. It still caused problems to the treatment works after they had been installed, and some effluent was still discharged into the river until the late 1950s.

Travel and Leisure
Along with the sort of day-outing organised by Strong's, the 1920s brought an increased popularity in rail travel. Many people now had paid holidays and were prepared to travel to coast and country. Romsonians were able to travel to Salisbury to connect with trains to many parts of the West Country. The

busy use of Romsey's rail station is indicated by the fact that there was a staff of 15 in 1927. Those who worked for the railway were entitled to cheap 'privilege' tickets for themselves and their families.

The 1920s also saw the development of road transport - private cars, commercial freight vehicles and public bus services run by various private companies. Coach, or charabanc, outings became popular. The increase in road traffic was recognised by Romsey Town Council, and the Railway Committee, set up in 1904, became the Road and Rail Committee in 1922.

A new open space appeared in Romsey during the 1920s when Colonel Wilfrid Ashley of Broadlands bought the land now called the South Garth, and restored it to Romsey Abbey. This land had long been private property, mainly as part of the very large garden of Abbotsford House (No 10 Market Place, now a bank). It was during this decade, in 1922, that Colonel Ashley's elder daughter, Edwina, married the future Lord Louis Mountbatten, great-grandson of Queen Victoria. His cousin the Prince of Wales acted as best man, and the newly married couple went on to lead a glamorous life in a blaze of publicity. They mixed with the 'aristocracy' of Hollywood's new film industry.

In Romsey, the new public entertainment of moving pictures was first provided in the old Corn Exchange and at the *Elite* cinema in Middlebridge Street, the *Elite* having been converted from an old wool-warehouse. This was the time of silent films, accompanied by suitable music on the piano. Romsey pianist, Mrs Barrett, played there in 1925. She had to arrange her own music, judging the type of story by the stars playing in it. Romantic pictures merited Strauss and Brahms; cowboy and adventure films were matched with overtures, whilst stirring marches were played for the news. She recalled:

> 'When a film of the Great War was being shown the manager decided this merited special treatment and engaged Mr Dunn, a member of the Romsey Town Band, to supply the effects. A curtain was rigged up in front of the screen and the bugler ensconced behind it with a bugle, an upturned galvanised bath and a drum and two sticks (I was creating havoc with the 1812 overture). All went well till the last night and we really had

204

excelled ourselves. We had the last bugle call, the last drum roll, the sticks came up with a flourish and down came the curtain! Poor Mr Dunn, covered in perspiration, galvanised bath and all; a bit of an anti-climax, but we won the war.'

Drawing by R. Watkinson, 1909-1997

In December 1931, the *Plaza* cinema opened at the Winchester Road/Southampton Road junction - a new cinema in a new building. It continued to provide film entertainment for some forty years.

Following Captain Suckling's death in 1922, the Romsey Golf Club moved to its present course at Rownhams. The Romsey Tennis Club played on courts in Harrage Park (now The Harrage) between the wars. The late Mrs Aldyth Wellington remembered the Club as more than a country town 'pat-and-tat' affair. Its grass courts were considered the best outside Wimbledon'. Football was played in various fields between the wars, and a recreation ground was leased to the Borough Council by Broadlands estate.

After 1938 the swimming area in Fishlake Stream was no longer needed because a purpose-built swimming pool was opened adjacent to the Crosfield Hall. The Hall itself was a gift to the town by Mr and Mrs J.J. Crosfield of Embley, and was built in 1936 on land 'provided by Lord Mount Temple [Wilfrid Ashley] on most generous terms' according to the newspaper account. The pool was also given to the town by Mr and Mrs Crosfield to commemorate the coronation of King George VI.

Health, Sanitation and Local Government

As World War I was ending, facilities at the Romsey's nursing home-cum-hospital were improved, and a contributory scheme was introduced to back up the voluntary support. The premises, now in the newly named Greatbridge Road, struggled on for a while. By the 1930s, however, the building was considered too small, and early in that decade a brand new Romsey & District Cottage Hospital was built on Mile Hill (now Winchester Hill). There were no permanent facilities for isolating victims of contagious diseases in Romsey, but the portable shepherds' huts, previously used effectively after an outbreak of smallpox, were still available.

Annual town health reports became obligatory after the First World War, and the report for the year 1920 by the local Medical Officer of Health, Dr Ralph Bartlett, gives a fascinating insight into the state of Romsey's health and sanitation.

He assessed Romsey's health to be generally superior to that of similar communities, about three quarters of the population being supplied with good piped water and the rest relying on wells. Although the water was hard, from percolation through chalk beds, the calcium content prevented poisonous lead compounds from the supply pipes dissolving into the water. He considered that the low-income houses were of poor design but well built and dry with large back yards, having 'outside sanitation which is good under the circumstances'.

By that time, half the houses were served by proper underground sewers feeding into the River Test via a precipitation tank, and the remainder, comprising some 577 closets, by the collection service. The operation of the precipitation tank, however, was not without its problems. The beneficial biological activity that took place in the tank was regularly disrupted by an inflow of coal tar acid from the Romsey gas works, which shared the same drainage system. The bacteria in the tank did not take kindly to being doused with such a powerful antiseptic (disinfectant).

In 1925 the Corporation Highways and Sanitary Committee took up the case for improving sewage disposal, and in 1926 a public meeting was held to review the proposed new drainage

scheme.   Burgesses on the register of electors were
vote on the proposals. Despite support at the public meet... _
the Borough Council elections were fought on the issue of
sewerage and, because of fears about increased rates, 'the
buckets' won.

In 1927 the Highways and Sanitary Committee of the Borough
Council was still discussing the rather sordid matter of the
buckets. 'Men have difficulty in getting through some houses
to remove buckets - suggest that each full bucket is replaced
by a clean one and that each bucket should have a lid'.

As well as being the dumping ground for the night-soil
collections, Budds Lane was the destination for all collected
household waste.   There it was sorted and all combustible
material 'at once fired'. Suitable unwanted material was used
as hard-core for road tracks and similar locations, but the
remaining debris was a magnet for a most unwelcome species
of wild life.   In 1924 'the police served the Town Clerk with
notice in respect of rats in the Sanitary Fields'. Efforts were
then made to find a suitable site for the proposed new sewage
farm.   An ideal site had been identified as early as 1903, but
could not be purchased so sewage collection continued.

In 1929, however, the Ministry of Health stepped in, requiring a
comprehensive drainage scheme to be put in at once. By this
time the cost had naturally escalated. In 1930 a public enquiry
was held to assess an application by Romsey Town Council for
a loan of £47,400 towards the construction of a sewage
disposal farm. Sanction for the loan was given but two years
later a second enquiry had to consider a further loan application
for £10,500 to cover 'excess expenditure'. The sewage farm
was duly commissioned at the bottom of Green Hill, and with
certain enlargements and modernisations, notably in the 1960s
and the mid-1980s, has served the town ever since.

In 1929, further local government reorganisation united the
rural district councils of Romsey and Stockbridge. A building to
house their officers was erected in Duttons Road. These district
councils were responsible for many local services such as road
repairs (other than main roads), sanitation, drainage, street
lighting, refuse collection and housing.

Education

Another responsibility that was to increase throughout the 20th century was that of the health of schoolchildren. This was achieved in a variety of ways, including medical and dental inspections, improved school sanitation, physical education, and school meals. The regular appearance of the 'nit' nurse, diligently searching for head lice, was viewed with foreboding, particularly by the girls. The provision of school milk, introduced in 1934 and lasting until the 1970s, was much more welcome. The net result of all these initiatives, popular or unpopular, was a much healthier generation of children, able to benefit more profitably from the education offered to them.

With a growing population, there was now considerable over-crowding in the schools. In 1923 the Council School - the one-time British School - achieved a much needed growth of premises. Infants and juniors stayed in the old buildings in The Hundred, opposite the Alma Road turning, and the older pupils moved to the new Senior School behind Plaza Parade in Winchester Road (now the site of Romsey Infant School). Unfortunately, the buildings were 'temporary' huts, mostly ex-military, and not replaced for some 30 years.

The nuns of La Sagesse Convent continued to run St Joseph's Orphanage. In 1923 *The Romsey Advertiser* commented that:

> 'an average of 60 to 70 boys are now filling the buildings every year. They have splendid premises, large airy dormitories, also for recreation a large playing field, gymnasium and an open air swimming baths. Three hundred boys have now passed through the orphanage. There is also a boarding school and day school attached to the Convent at which there are about 80 pupils.'

In the next decades ideas on child-care changed, and the orphanage closed. It was not to be the only change of attitude. As the country approached the tumult of the World War II, Romsey was unaware that the tenor and pace of its life would soon be altered out of all recognition. The era of front-room shops, of errand boys and individual businesses was coming to an end.

THE SECOND WORLD WAR

Preparations were well in hand some time before the outbreak of war in 1939. Every household in the country was circulated with a Home Office booklet entitled 'Protection of Your Home against Air Raids', and gas masks were distributed. By mid-May 1938 even the schools were issued with notes on anti-gas training for the use of teachers. These notes contained descriptions of the effects of different types of gases and how to prevent contamination.

Romsey Extra Parish Council minutes are probably indicative of what was going on all over the country:

24.3.38 Military Manoeuvres will be carried out in the district for 3 months from 1 July 1938.

19.1.39 Govt. Evacuation scheme - Council to appoint visitors to make house to house survey to ascertain accommodation available for the reception of children in event of an emergency.

19.5.39 Evacuation - In the event of emergency Romsey Extra would receive 153 unaccompanied children, 15 teachers and helpers and 225 others; total 393. Council to nominate a Billeting Officer who would be responsible for completing and issuing a form to each householder on whom evacuees are billeted, and this would be used to obtain maintenance allowance paid by Government.

By 1st September 1939, blackout had become compulsory; gasmasks and identity cards had been issued and had to be carried. No lights were permitted in the streets, and only a glimmer of blue light in trains. On 2nd September 1939 - the day before the declaration of war - Air Raid Precautions (ARP) volunteers were mobilised. Large factories and offices were required to provide ARP volunteers from their own staff, whilst the towns and villages set up Parish Warden posts.

Mobilisation Order No 1 for Romsey Borough & Romsey Rural District, dated 2nd September, indicated that one mobile unit (duties unspecified) had its HQ at Chirk Lodge and there were First Aid parties with headquarters at Mitchell's Garage and Duke's Mill (old Town Mill) as well as other locations. ARP posts were set up at various points, including Strong's Brewery and the town hall.

The ARP wardens' duties included making sure that the public were directed to shelters when a warning was sounded, and that there were no lights showing anywhere after dark. The volunteers included people of all ages and classes. Boy Scouts were used as mock casualties for Civil Defence First Aid Training and as messengers at the Warden Posts.

Just a few days before the outbreak of war the first evacuees arrived in the Romsey area. Children, expectant mothers and invalids were moved from Gosport, Portsmouth and Southampton into the Romsey district and beyond. On 1st and 2nd September there were three special trains to Romsey and one to Dunbridge each day. The railways were very busy with many other trains passing through Romsey. Volunteers from organisations like the Women's Voluntary Service (WVS) were in much demand, helping to ease the difficult and frightening situation for suddenly uprooted travellers.

It was not easy for either the evacuee children or their foster parents, and because there were no immediate threats of air raids many children went home. By Christmas, three months after the start of the war, a large proportion had done so.

The railway continued to be very busy throughout the war. In December 1939 King George VI visited all the naval dockyards in the country, and Romsey's claim to fame is that he spent the night in his train in the upside yard of Romsey Station whilst travelling from Devonport to Portsmouth.

Food rationing was in force by early 1940, and people were encouraged to cultivate their gardens, growing vegetables in every available space. Dr Lalonde had a pig in the garden of his home at Wykeham House, and hens, ducks and geese on the tennis court there. Rationing involved both the authorities and the shopkeepers with extra bureaucracy at a time when they were becoming increasingly short of staff.

In order to help with the food shortages, and to enable more women to take on full-time jobs and men to work longer hours, most factories established canteens supplying meals at low prices. And to help those who had no access to such food the Government set up British Restaurants to supplement food rations in most towns. Romsey's British Restaurant was established in the hall belonging to the United Reformed Church and was staffed by the WVS. It continued to function for several years after the war - a service that was much appreciated whilst some foods were still rationed. By then it was managed by the Town Council and called the Civic Restaurant.

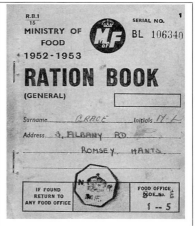

Rationing continued until 1953
Reference: LTVAS Grace Collection

The retreat from Dunkirk, in 1940, was a shock to the country, but there was little time to dwell on this dark moment of the war because life became very busy. Returning soldiers were billeted all over the town - in empty buildings, halls, or the upstairs rooms of pubs. Newly erected houses in Alma Road were taken over. The Corn Exchange housed a NAAFI - the Navy Army & Air Force Institute - which functioned as a canteen or club room for service men and women. Other rest rooms were run by the Baptist and Methodist congregations. The Scout Headquarters in Church Street, which had been part of the old Lansdowne Arms, was used by the military for the duration of the war. Test House, off Mill Lane, accommodated various sections of the military for most of the war. There was a cookhouse for one section in Newton Lane.

By the summer following the evacuation of British troops from Dunkirk, the war had become more real, and the country had to face up to the possibility of invasion. Romsey began to make preparations, for it was thought that the Germans might land at Eastleigh airport as well as driving inland from the coast. There were many forms of defence.

In one house in Botley Road a machine-gun post was set up in the front bedroom. On the Southampton road, by the entry to what is now Knatchbull Close, a defence post was established in the big oak tree - there is still an iron bar up in the branches - and portable road blocks were ready by the roadside. Just off the road at Greatbridge there are still the remains of blocks once placed to help prevent tanks crossing the bridge.

Home Guard parade c1944
The sergeant is Mr Powell, father of LTVAS member Meg Powell

Men who were either too young or too old to join the Armed Services, or were in a reserved occupation, joined the Local Defence Volunteers (LDV), later renamed the Home Guard. In the early years they worked alongside Army personnel guarding railway bridges and other key points in case of invasion through Eastleigh Aerodrome. One of their number commented afterwards that there were various ammunition dumps around the town - in the Drill Hall and at Moody's gunshop in Church Street. 'We spent a lot of time moving ammunition about, and it seems likely that Romsey was more in danger of accidental fire setting alight some of this ammunition than from enemy bombing.'

212

As the war progressed, more men and women left their peace-time jobs to join the Armed Services or become full-time Civil Defence members. The Civil Defence was a new concept, and included the Auxiliary Fire Service, which later became part of the National Fire Service. Romsey's Fire Station was then in the Hundred, on the site of the old Hundred Brewery, now Wakeford Court. Later in the war it moved to Latimer Street, near the junction with Portersbridge Street, only settling in its present location in Alma Road in the 1960s. In the villages around Romsey, individuals often filled more than one role. At Michelmersh the headmaster of the school wore several hats - he was a special constable, he was in the Home Guard, and the Fire Service trolley was stored on his premises.

While there was little local demand for the services of these special groups, some were called in to help with problems elsewhere. Romsey only suffered minor damage during the air war that followed the retreat from France in the summer of 1940, but it was very different in Southampton.

The people of Southampton suffered a great deal and many left their town every night. Those seeking refuge in Romsey were taken in by local householders. Some eventually made their home in the town: some made lifelong friends. Southampton bus drivers used to drive their buses full of people out of Southampton at night. One bus parked in Bridge Road, a quiet street off Winchester Road near the Botley Road junction. Another, whose driver lived at Awbridge, carried its passengers there nightly for safety. The passengers slept in the bus or with local people and returned to Southampton in the morning. The men's mess room at Wills Nursery was able to accommodate 33 of these 'nightly refugees'.

One particular Southampton misfortune had an unexpected positive effect on Romsey. In 1941 Smith Bradbeer & Co. Ltd arrived from Southampton, where their premises had received a direct hit from a bomb. Initially, they took premises in the Market Place, and no-one at the time appreciated that they were to become part of the town's long-term history.

In Romsey, Middlebridge House, near the far end of Middlebridge Street, was demolished and a bomb fell on Green

Hill, where it remained unexploded for a time. When it was detonated by the Army, it caused some slight damage to the Tool House and Engine House at the sewage works.

At the Brewery, Air Raid Precautions included duties at night. A personal memory of a newly married young lady, who worked in the bottling plant, recalled ARP duties. One involved dealing with incendiary bombs, small devices which could be extinguished with what was known as a stirrup pump. A jet of water was propelled against the fire, the water being pumped from a bucket.

> 'About six of us used to go on Night Watch in Strong's offices. It was nerve racking. We used to make our beds there, taking our own sheets and pillow cases. We had mattresses on the floor. When the sirens went we had to go to the yard to see there were no incendiaries falling. The gun fire was terrible but that was our own guns. The noise was so loud you thought they were in the yard with you. We had a little bit of training. If any incendiary came down you had to lay on the ground and spray them.'

People were on night watch in other parts of Romsey.

Whenever a warning sounded at the approach of enemy aircraft over the south coast, most people took shelter. The children at the Abbey School marched quickly from school into the Abbey. The children from the Convent were considered safe in an underground tunnel used to keep children dry when going from one school building to another. Those who went to school in what is now the Infants school behind Plaza Parade took shelter in the *Plaza* cinema, an alarmingly obvious large white building but with no windows - shattering glass was a great danger.

Several people remember low-flying German planes machine-gunning across the town during the daytime. They smashed a large amount of Wills Nursery glass - but overall the damage during the war was not great. It was thought that the German pilots preferred not to destroy the glasshouses, which were a useful landmark clearly visible from 20 miles away.

Several aircraft crashed in the area. In August 1940 two German aircraft crashed on consecutive days, one in

214

Broadlands Park and one at East Dean. The airmen were buried in Romsey Cemetery, the RAF supplying the transport and the bearers. The bodies were exhumed in the 1960s and buried at a German War Cemetery in the Midlands. Other wounded German airmen were treated at Romsey Hospital.

There is a note in the minutes of the Highways and Sanitary Committee that says that two houses in Love Lane were being used by persons de-housed by enemy action. There is also a note saying that the Corporation must be refunded for the expenses incurred for disinfestation and cleansing of the County Senior School after it had been used for housing refugees.

A few quotes from the minutes of the Corporation Highways & Sanitary Committee of late 1940 and early 1941 are evocative.

> 1940 June 6   Mortuary accommodation to be arranged for air raid casualties - Cub Hut, Mill Lane. To be used as Cub Hut until required.
> 1940 Sept 5 Bakeries to keep enough water on premises for 48 hrs use - in case of air raid damage to water mains
> 1941 April 3   Park railings taken down to be sold at best price, for use for munitions.

Churchyard railings had also been taken by 5th June.   On receiving a complaint by Mr Talbot that his railing had been damaged, it was decided to tell him they were scheduled for removal. (It seems to have been unwise to complain.) At this time, general household metal was collected in the playground of the boys' school in Station Road.

> 1942 March 5   Cleansing facilities for Scabies - Cleansing centre [erected in case of poisonous gas attacks] in Love Lane is at present being used for cleansing military personnel - could be used also for scabies.   Only required if large outbreak - at present Poor Law Institution can cope.

By November 1942 scabies was being treated in Southampton.

Harefield House - its grounds later to be developed as Viney Avenue - became the home of No 210 Maintenance Unit of the RAF until 1946. The house had been built in the 19th century by Thomas Strong of the Strong's Brewery family.   The

215

gatehouse or lodge to the property served as the Guard room; it still stands on the corner of Viney Avenue with the A3090.

The main house had a large ballroom that was used as the dining room, while the main administrative offices and kitchens were in the rest of the house. The WAAF cooks slept in the main house but the others had quarters at Abbotswood House on the Braishfield Road. The men slept at Highwood House (Stroud School). Outside in the grounds were various huts, used for storing the materials that were the units' work.

> 'We handled everything from nuts & bolts to aircraft, uniforms to socks pants & shoes, sheet metal, engines to blankets. One Boxing Day we had to empty 99 wagons from Romsey Station. We delivered to 66 aerodromes or depots - to name a few, Ford, Tangmere, Thorney Island, Chichester, Gosport, Priddys Hard, Portsmouth, Titchfield, Havant, Calshot, Upavon, Netheravon, Stoney Cross, Andover, Middle Wallop, Eastleigh, Tarrant Rushton, Bournemouth.'

Service people relaxing on the lawn of Harefield House

The Service people joined in the life of the town; they held dances with their own band and other entertainments. The WAAF played netball against Romsey schoolgirls - the Romsey girls felt it a bit unfair to be playing against adults. Sometimes an Army band played in the Abbey.

216

Meanwhile the town's shops and workplaces continued to function. Mr Summers, the headmaster, died in 1942 and Osborne House School closed, but the building was reopened by the County Council to cope with the influx of evacuees. For several years, crocodiles of pupils from other schools processed to Osborne House where a hut was used for school lunches.

The Chairman and Managing Director of Strong's Brewery, Mr Chambers, served as Mayor throughout the war, just as Mr Bowen had in the previous conflict. He had many extra responsibilities, including those of overseeing the Civil Defence and supervising the settlement of evacuees. He also had to cope with numerous day-to-day problems at the Brewery as more and more members of the male staff were called up.

The management of the Brewery had to deal with a more acute staff shortage than most because some seventy employees had joined the Territorial Army in 1938 and were thus amongst the first to be called up. For a time, Mr Chambers also had to deal with the logistics of aircraft stored in the lorry garages at the Horsefair site. He must have been relieved that, in common with most of Romsey, the Brewery escaped war damage.

More pleasurable for him was a contribution made by the Brewery towards the end of the war. In July 1944, a month after the D-Day invasion of northern France, Spitfires flew supplies of Strong's beer to troops in Normandy, in casks suspended from each wing. A blind eye was turned to this unofficial operation, which was listed as 'XXX Depth Charge Fitment'. It is worth noting that the Brewery was very busy throughout the war, brewing seven days a week even with their depleted staff.

Some places either added special war work to their normal duties or changed altogether. Mitchell's Garage in Middlebridge Street continued to sell petrol, which was rationed and had no brand name. It was called Pool Petrol and in the opinion of Mr Alf Mitchell was more like paraffin. Having made shells during the First World War, Mitchell's now also made parts of 'Bailey' bridges. These were temporary prefabricated bridges made of steel, used by the Army whenever a quick river crossing was needed. The Rev. Berthon would have approved.

Rolfe's caravan business also turned to war work. Employees were busy repairing RAF and Army vehicles, making trailers, and other items such as firing pins for mortar guns and ramp plates for fixing to gliders. They also worked on tanks, fitting ducts to the exhaust systems so that the engines could still run as the vehicles disembarked from the landing craft and went ashore through the water.

The Test Valley Ironworks was still operating in the Hundred (now Lloyds the chemist). Their main business of repairing agricultural machinery was very essential work to the war effort as no new items were being made. Hattat's Jam Factory, the home of the Hampshire Preserving Company, continued to make jam and canned goods for the armed forces.

Arthur Wills at the 'tomato factory' was an astute reader of the signs of the times. Although it was not a rifle that he took up this time to go to war, he led an efficient food-producing organisation, which, at a critical time, rapidly expanded production of essential food crops, grown not only under intensive glasshouse conditions but also under extensive outdoor cultivation. Tadburn Nursery remained the H.Q. and control centre for this enhanced production, which was now supported by the newly completed Shelley Nursery at Ower and other recently acquired nurseries and farms.

Included in the enlarged holding were the water meadows at Fishlake, below the Barge Canal (the local name for the old canal). Dutch engineers were brought in to advise on the drainage and pumping of the area, and labour for the work was provided by the Land Army and German prisoners of war from Ganger Camp. The land was then used initially for potatoes and later for cereals. One weekend during the war the only potatoes available to buy in Southampton were those supplied by Wills.

As well as improving production within his own business, Mr Wills devoted himself to the duties shouldered in his capacity as a member of the Hampshire County War Agricultural Executive Committee. He was closely involved in the committee's endeavours to raise the output of essential food crops and livestock everywhere.

D-Day

Preparations for D-Day, which marked the start of the liberation of Europe, meant the presence of even more troops in the area. Romsey Station was an important link for the transport of troops and goods assembling during this preparation period.

American servicemen now arrived in large numbers. They were as popular with the local girls as they were with other war-rationed communities; in their impressively stylish uniforms they were often a source of luxuries such as nylon stockings and chocolates.

Some Americans had already set up a large camp at Lockerley just west of Dunbridge Station to store and distribute Lease-Lend materials. As the war progressed, the area taken over by the American troops was enlarged, and eventually 130 sheds were erected, and railway lines and a platform were added to the complex. In *Springboard for Overlord*, Anthony Kemp explains that the United States Army Transportation Corps played a large part in organising the shipment of men and materials from Southampton docks after D-Day. This required much work beforehand. Around Southampton, several large camps were set up which were totally self-contained. In the immediate vicinity of Romsey, Broadlands Camp was known as Camp C15 on Area C Sub-area 7. An American contingent shared the responsibility for the administration and guarding of Area C, and had their H.Q. at Ampfield House.

Within Romsey, most of Broadlands house itself was used as an annexe of the Royal South Hants Hospital. Cupernham House in Woodley Lane (site of Carisbrook Court) was equipped as an annexe for the Southampton Eye Hospital. The railway station siding served a vital role as the base for an improvised hospital train that picked up wounded servicemen from local ports.

The Bypass was closed, and British troops camped there with cans of fuel to supply convoys from more distant parts as they passed through Romsey. In Alma Road there were troops in the Council houses that had been completed just before the war but not yet occupied. At the back of Station Road, there was a camp in the paddock off Orchard Lane, currently occupied by the farmers' trading co-operative, SCATS.

219

Although the American Army embarked from Dorset beaches for the initial attack, Romsonians can remember them in the Romsey area before D-Day. A considerable number of contingents were well concealed against the wall of Broadlands Park along the By-pass, where military numbering still survives. Others were camped by the roadside along the Straight Mile, the A3090 to Winchester just beyond Crampmoor. Black troops were stationed on one side and white on the other, and Romsonians witnessed several fights.

The American troops were more generously supplied with food, cigarettes, sweets, etc. than the British. On one occasion, they offered the RAF personnel of Harefield House a full barrel of beer after a dance at the Crosfield Hall, and the delighted British airmen rolled it all the way up Winchester Hill to their camp. One Romsonian who worked at the rubbish dump often brought home unopened tins of food thrown out by the American forces.

Prisoner of War Camps
As the tide of war began to turn, many prisoners of war were brought to the area. The first such group had a tented camp at Woodley on the west side of School Road. Later, there was a large hutted camp on the east side - known as Ganger Camp. Prisoners from the Italian and German Armed Services were housed there.

The Italians built and decorated a camp theatre, the decorations being made from flattened food tins, which they painted. Romsonians were employed by the camp's NAAFI, and one family still keeps in contact with prisoner friends made at the time. After the war temporary accommodation was required for many 'displaced persons' - people of all nationalities who had been moved about Europe by the Germans or escaped from their own countries. These included Poles, Ukrainians and Yugoslavs.

The prisoners captured from the German Army were very often of other nationalities because the Germans had forced people they captured in other countries to fight for them or to work for them. There was one captive requiring medical treatment whom nobody could understand. Finally, a Southampton

Docks' doctor was asked to help, since he had a small knowledge of many languages in order to treat venereal diseases amongst seamen. He discovered that the soldier came from a small Baltic island with a dialect spoken only on that island.

Prisoners were put to work in various places in Romsey including the Gas Works. The camp was guarded by the Pioneer Corps, but the prisoners were mostly young and not keen to escape. Indeed, some of them eventually chose to remain in this country. Several married local girls, and settled down with their new families to cope with the more congenial problems of peacetime.

In Remembrance

The sacrificial trench warfare of 1914-18 may not have been repeated in the Second World War, but it had its own traumas over six long years. Many local families suffered great loss, and 61 names were added to Romsey's war memorial.

A long familiar view as it appeared at the Millennium
Photographed by Charles Burnett

This view of the Market Place, taken in August 2000, shows the same aspect as that in the watercolour by the unknown artist, who stood at this spot in 1809 (see front cover). Bollards denoting the pedestrian area to the left have replaced the rails of the old Hundred Bridge, and the water of the Holbrook now runs under the road. Buildings have changed but the overall shape of the Market Place survives, and the Abbey church gazes over the far roof-tops as it has done for nearly 900 years.

1945 to the MILLENNIUM

Returning Heroes
Service men and women returned home. Among them was Lord Mountbatten, who in 1946 was given the freedom of the Borough of Romsey in acknowledgement of his vital role in the war. In return, he presented the town with one of the captured Japanese guns that he had brought back from Burma.

The euphoria over, everyone had to settle down to post-war austerity, and rebuild lives. A major need for the restoration of normality was an adequate provision of homes. Although Romsey had not suffered the housing loss of some towns, there was a shortage of accommodation for a booming population.

The Housing Boom
It seems that wars create a need for, and stir the conscience about, good housing for all. As in 1918, an explosion of building followed the Second World War. Just as the first Council housing projects were completed soon after the first World War, so housing was at the top of the agenda at Romsey Borough and Rural District Council meetings in 1945. This time the situation was aggravated by the loss of so many homes in the south of England, and by the scarcity of building materials. The problem had to be tackled with ingenuity.

Immediately after VE day, the military were asked by the Borough to de-requisition the houses erected just before the war in Alma Road. At the same time, June 1945, the Ministry of Health offered the Borough Council twenty temporary prefabricated bungalows. As men and women were demobbed from the Services, so the need for more housing became ever more pressing. The housing authorities found it necessary to requisition large empty properties.

People became desperate for somewhere to live and they took matters into their own hands. In October 1946, a few months after the final cessation of hostilities, *The Romsey Advertiser* reported a meeting of the Romsey & Stockbridge Rural District Council at which 'The Squatter Problem' was discussed. Various hutted camps had already been occupied by people desperate for accommodation.

One such site, named as the 'Luzborough Civil Defence Site', housed eleven families. The buildings were expected to last for five years. It was estimated that £400 would be needed to partition each hut, supply a kitchen range per dwelling and to treat the roofs. The existing kitchen premises could be used for communal washing and a similar use could be made of the shower hut. The rent agreed was 7s 6d per week for a complete hut, 5s 0d for half a hut. Similar camps were occupied at Woodley, and in Nursling, Baddesley, Chilworth and other parts of the rural district.

Both the Borough Council and the Rural District Council then started a busy housing programme. (This lasted until the Government decided in 1988 that local government should not be responsible for building houses.) Compulsory purchase orders were made on properties such as Harefield House on Winchester Hill and Test House in Mill Lane, as and when they were relinquished by the Armed Services in the months immediately following the end of the war. These properties could be converted into varied accommodation without too much expense. By Autumn 1946, the lodge, coachman's cottage and a bungalow at Harefield, together with converted flats at Test House, were all ready for occupation. This effort was followed by the erection of houses on what was known as the 'Botley Road site' and which became Chambers Avenue. Over the following years, Romsey Borough Council continued its housing programme at Priestlands and Harefield.

The Borough's pre-war housing area in Duttons Road and Malmesbury Road had started to extend to the east side of Alma Road before the war, and this was continued, though not without difficulty. The universal shortage of building materials and labour was complicated by opposition to the disappearance of the cricket pitch.

The Romsey Advertiser of 6th May 1948 had plenty to tell its readers on the subject of new homes:
> 'Another stage in Romsey's housing programme has been reached this week with the completion of the first of three pairs of bungalows being built by direct labour by the borough council as part of the Alma Road scheme.

The tenants have been chosen and will take up residence within the next few days, the occasion being marked by a little ceremony similar to that of a year ago when the first tenants took possession of the temporary bungalows in the Botley Road estate. Round the corner in Mountbatten Avenue progress has been made too, in the groups of houses being erected by local builders.

Perhaps the scene of the greatest housing activity locally is the Botley Road site, where work is in progress on the construction of 36 Reema houses.'

Reema was one of the various forms of prefabricated building developed at this time to speed the supply of houses. They were precast at North Baddesley by Reed & Mallick.

The next area to be developed was Priestlands. This site was another of Romsey's charity lands and was also the location for the new Romsey Secondary School. Apparently, Romsey Council was unaware that the site belonged to them until the Hampshire County Council decided to build the school.

Initially, the main type of domestic building was the two-storey house with garden, but, as the waiting lists stayed long and land became more difficult to obtain, the answer was considered to be flats. So it was that, in the 1960s, much of Banning Street disappeared, and Broadwater Road arrived with the distinctive blocks of flats on its south side.

The next development, in the following decade, was at Mercer Way, named after the long-serving head of the school that is now Romsey Junior School. The Mercer Way estate contained a mix of accommodation - flats, houses and bungalows.

In earlier times, sponsored housing for the elderly and infirm had been provided by private endowments of almshouses. Romsey's almshouses had only accommodated a small minority, usually women. In the second half of the 20th century suitable accommodation for more of the elderly and infirm, male and female, was considered to be as essential a duty of the new Welfare State as housing for families.

225

'Sheltered Accommodation' became the name of various forms of housing. As its name implies, the occupants were provided with support from a warden who looked after the administration of the block and was the first port of call if help was needed. Romsey acquired several blocks, Linden Court in Linden Road being the first to be built in 1969, and administered by the local Council. A similar smaller establishment was built on the south-west corner of the new Broadwater Road as a memorial to Lady Edwina Mountbatten of Broadlands. She had died in 1960 while carrying out an overseas tour on behalf of the St John's Ambulance Brigade. The Edwina Mountbatten House is administered by a trust, and houses retired Hampshire people.

1973 saw the beginning of a new trend - the sale of Council houses to sitting tenants, and by the end of the century local government controlled housing was being moved to the administration of private housing trusts. *The Romsey Advertiser* of 23rd March 1973 reported:

'No 27 Tadfield Crescent, Romsey's first council house to be sold. Sold on March 2 for £7,200'

The clearance of old unfit houses, which had begun before the war, continued afterwards with the enthusiastic aim of providing good quality housing for everyone. The move to renovate old buildings rather than demolish them was only set in train when the Romsey & District Society was formed in 1974. At that time Love Lane, Banning Street, Newton Lane and Middlebridge Street had lost old houses. Several in Cherville Street were about to be demolished. The change in local government had made the town hall a redundant building and there was talk of replacing it with a modern office block. In 1975 the Romsey & District Society established the Romsey and District Buildings Preservation Trust, which has been able to save a variety of properties, buying, renovating and then re-selling them.

The latter half of the 20th century saw the greatest increase of population and with it the change from the small local builder, who erected up to a dozen houses 'on spec', to the national development company which planned and built whole estates with roads, open spaces, and designated plots for shops and schools. The areas of Cupernham, Woodley, Whitenap and

Halterworth, which had formerly been separate hamlets of farmland with few houses, now accommodated great numbers of newcomers to the area, many of whom chose to live in Romsey although working elsewhere.

The growth of the town during most of the 20th century was mainly to the east of the historic centre with the exception of developments at Rivermead and Riverside Gardens in the 1960s and 1970s. At last, in the final decade of the century, building finally spread to the ancient water-meadows known as Fishlake Meadows, in an area to the north of the old town not previously considered suitable for building.

Changing Times and Changing Industries
In the years following the end of the Second World War, Romsey underwent other changes besides that of population and housing. Several of the businesses that had been part and fabric of town life came to an end.

Although the Romsey Gas Company had struggled valiantly throughout the war and had doubled its 1915 figure of 730 customers by 1949, it fell victim to nationalisation. The installation was too out-of-date to warrant continuation in the modernised industry, and gas was supplied from Southampton. The town's two gasholders were taken down in the mid-1950s and the town supplied by natural gas in 1974.

The Jam Factory was another casualty. After the war, people's tastes changed and the standard of living rose. Meat and savouries replaced jam at teatime and the Romsey factory could not compete with the larger companies. It closed in 1960, and the derelict building later fell victim to a disastrous fire.

Romsey
CHOICE
STRAWBERRY
JAM
The Hampshire Preserving Co. Ltd., Romsey

By permission of
Hampshire Record Office
Reference: HRO 2M92
from collection deposited by
Mr J.H. Armstrong

The Test Valley Ironworks closed soon after the jam factory. The business had declined between the two World Wars. Although it showed a slight improvement during the 1940s - when three Italian prisoners of war from Ganger Camp were employed - it finally closed in 1962.

Perhaps the most telling end in historical terms was the closing of the cattle market in Newton Lane. With this closure in 1966 the long tradition of Romsey's great medieval market was virtually over. Only a small general market held every Friday and Saturday in the yard of the *Dolphin Hotel* now survives as a faint echo of former glories.

Label from one of the most popular brews

After 1955 Strong & Co. Ltd was an associate of Whitbread's, with Whitbread directors sitting on Strong's Board. In 1969 Whitbread's acquired the whole company, uniting with Strong & Co. Ltd of Romsey and Brickwoods of Portsmouth, to become Whitbread Wessex Ltd in 1973. By this time both machinery and working practices at the Horsefair Brewery needed to be modernised if they were to continue. A decision was taken against this investment and the Horsefair Brewery was then gradually run down. It ceased brewing in 1981, ceased processing and kegging in 1987 and closed finally in 1990. By 1999 some of the buildings had been converted into offices, some remained empty and much of the site had been cleared, awaiting development.

Mr Fred Aldred was probably typical of the Romsonians who worked at the Brewery. He started work at the Engineer's store in 1930 at the age of 14. He stayed with the company for 44 years - rising to Chief Engineer's Clerk, responsible for a vast variety of items covering all departments of the Brewery.

It is not possible to overstate the influence Strong's had on Romsey. With the last of the mergers in 1965 Strong's Group controlled 920 licensed houses. Many families spent all their working lives at the Brewery, which long provided regular if not very well paid work. Most employees lived within walking or cycling distance, returning home for dinner. Strong's owned and built houses near the Brewery for some staff.

The Brewery also supported the town in many ways. The Fire Brigade was mainly staffed by men from the Brewery, being not too far from successive fire stations in Church Street, Latimer Street and finally Alma Road.

Mr A.R. Wills, the tomato grower, died in 1949 and the nursery had two new directors, his son Mr A.J. Wills and Mr Reg Leeman. There was much new work to put in hand, sterilising the soil which had suffered from intensive cropping of tomatoes, and rethinking the heating system.

In the 1960s around 200 people were employed at the nursery. In 1962 Wills' Tadburn Nursery added a completely new unit in the form of 'The Garden Centre', which provided a fresh and novel outlet for its own widening range of products and that of other holdings. It started as a modest pioneer effort in direct selling to the public. The venture progressed rapidly, with the potential to help satisfy the nation's demand for 'instant all-the-year-round' gardening, utilising the many advantages of container grown plants in a great variety of species.

The business was very much a community with management operating an 'open door' policy that paid off. Long service was common, with some employees serving 50 years, and the business was one of the first in the industry to offer a contributory pension scheme to its employees. There was a charge-hand for each acre of tomatoes, and regular meetings of charge-hands were held to meet staff and discuss matters of policy and other technical or staff issues. Leading growers, members of the staffs of the Ministry of Agriculture research and demonstration stations, representatives from wholesale markets, as well as suppliers of equipment, were frequently invited to attend the meetings. The company's contribution to the technical development urgently needed for the future health of the horticultural industry became highly regarded.

The major part of the company went into liquidation in 1983 when the business comprised Tadburn Nursery at Romsey, Shelley Nursery at Ower and Nethercourt Nursery at

Pennington.   The Garden Centre was sold to Hillier's, the present owners.

One business project that took a change of direction was Rolfe's. A serious fire at the Caravan works in 1950 started a decline in this aspect of work. Continuing its garage business, the company then diversified into garden machinery for some years, and later, in the last decade of the century, combined the garage with a small supermarket.

Yet, while old established businesses were coming to the end of their long life, several new industries were starting. In the 1950s, Romsey followed fashion, and industrial estates were set up in Budds Lane and at Belbins with purpose-built industrial buildings. Part of the Budds Lane site had been the town's rubbish dump in earlier days and land at Belbins had been used for gravel and sand extraction.

Further industrial sites followed - Romsey Industrial Estate on the east side of Greatbridge Road, and Abbey Park on the south-east side of the town between Romsey and North Baddesley, and two on Yokesford Hill, north of the town. The Romsey Industrial Estate has 56 sites listed on its information board and the other large estates cater for similar numbers. There were also numerous small developments in disused farm buildings in the countryside around the town. These catered for small businesses covering a great variety of activities. Over the forty years since the first of these developments many industries have been developed but not all have stayed.

One of the most important tenants at Budds Lane in 1966 was Hampshire Industrial Textiles, better known as the 'Carpet Factory'. It started with 20 employees. By 1974, 250 people worked for the company, some on the original site and others in an additional building on the other side of Greatbridge Road. Then the company became part of the Wilton Royal Carpet Company, which was itself taken over, and by 1995 it had closed. Many other businesses, however, continue to thrive.

Romsey's industries now cover a very wide field from brewing, cabinet making, computer technology in many forms, industrial cleaning, express deliveries, to printing, sheet metal working, used car sales, and vehicle repairing. Amongst these are small organisations concentrating on a specialised branch of their industry or working on entirely new ideas.

Shops
After the Second World War, the style of shops and shopping began to change almost imperceptibly. At first there were many young 14-18 year old lads available for low-paid work while awaiting call-up for National Service, but gradually, as this obligation was phased out, so jobs such as 'errand boy' also faded from the scene. The only home delivery came from the mail-order companies that became very popular. Small 'self-service' shops evolved into supermarkets. Then came hypermarkets with the Internet just around the corner in the 21st century.

Instead of the dozen or so butchers in Romsey at the beginning of the 20th century, only two independent butchers remain in the year 2000. Stares the butchers have survived over five generations on one site, and a butcher's shop, now owned by Mr Drummond, has been on the corner of Cornmarket and Bell Street since the late 1800s.

Since the 1950s, furniture stores have gradually stopped keeping stocks of large items, or making their own, but have simply acted as ordering agents for manufacturers so that the customer may have to wait for an order to come through. Many Romsey people turn to the furniture department now within Bradbeer's when they look for major household items. In 1946, the company moved to Bell Street from its emergency wartime location in the Market Place.

The Bell Street shop was purchased from Messrs Percy and Frank Leach, and reconstructed to open as Smith Bradbeer's Fashion Showroom. The store prospered until 1963 when it had one of the worst fires experienced in Romsey. The adjacent Bell Furnishing Stores was also damaged. Both properties were subsequently restored; in 1969 the Furnishing Store was incorporated with the Fashion Showroom and an upper storey was added to the building. 1997 saw the 160th anniversary of the foundation of Mr R.C. Smith's Drapery Store in Southampton.

231

Along with other outlets for women's clothes, Smith Bradbeer's has seen many changes in fashion, such as the disappearance of all too easily snagged silk stockings in favour of nylon, and the advent of tights instead of stockings as a direct result of the revolution that was the mini-skirt.

All types of shops were affected by changes to packaging with the general use of modern wrapping as opposed to paper and cardboard. This made a tremendous difference to the grocery trade - goods such as sugar, tea, butter, margarine and biscuits could be pre-wrapped at the point of manufacture and no longer individually dispensed in Romsey's grocery shops. Steam-baked bread, pre-wrapped in plastic, came in during the 1950s. The days of old-style grocers such as Purchase's, Hook Brothers, Pink's, Brown's, the International and the Home & Colonial were numbered.

The introduction of refrigerators and then freezers had a tremendous impact; commercial freezers permitted a whole new way of preparing food, whilst domestic fridge/freezers brought a transformation in shopping patterns. No longer was it necessary to buy fresh food daily.

Supermarkets began to spread about that time. They revolutionised shopping and increasingly ousted many of the individual shops, although Romsey did not have a supermarket until Waitrose arrived on the old Jam Factory site in 1969.

In 1986 Romsey's shops were suffering the same difficulties as the rest of the country. There were then 16 empty shops in the town. By 1988, however, that number had reduced to nine. This was the period of considerable change in the occupancy of the town's shops. The first charity shop, Oxfam, arrived in 1986 and by 1988 there were nine estate agents. Greetings card shops also became popular; they offered inexpensive gifts as well as cards.

Transport
In the 1950s the first of the post-war road improvements again focused on the main road leaving Romsey for the west. This time a sharp bend at the bottom of Pauncefoot Hill was

straightened out, and the turning into the A27 Whiteparish road was improved. Pauncefoot Hill itself became a relatively gradual gradient with a two-lane dual carriage way.

The decades after the Second World War saw a fast growth in both commercial and private road traffic. Many Romsonians still remember long tailbacks of traffic on summer weekends as the rest of the world travelled west down Winchester Hill, along the Bypass and over Middlebridge. The building of the M27 gave much relief to the beleaguered town of Romsey, which still suffers if the motorway is closed for any reason.

The 1960s, when car ownership became more widespread, saw railway closures. The Andover to Redbridge service via Romsey ceased in 1964 and part of the track north of Romsey was turned into a public footpath in 1974. The passenger service from Romsey to Eastleigh came to an end in 1969, although the track continued to be used for regular freight services and for emergency use when the Southampton tunnel was out of action. At the end of the 20th century Hampshire County Council was anxious that this line should be used more fully and was supporting a move to re-open Chandlers Ford railway station.

The Victorian rail bridges became a source of trouble for the large commercial vehicles now on the roads. 1972 saw a very bad accident when a car was crushed by a container that was ripped off a lorry going under the bridge at the *Sun Inn*. It took some time before a system of diverting high vehicles finally came into being.

Meanwhile, the bus services had improved and in 1972 a new bus station was opened off Broadwater Road. (The first discussion about removing buses from the Market Place had been aired at a Borough Council Meeting in 1947.)

By the end of the 20th century attitudes had changed again, and private motorists were being encouraged to use public transport. Schemes were promoted to free town centres from traffic. The Cornmarket became a pedestrian area, and discussions were under way to improve the passenger access to railway stations. A bus service was introduced offering a direct link to Winchester railway station for transport to London. The town's existing car parks were still very busy, though, and the anticipated building of a new supermarket in the town centre was expected to change the pattern of traffic and the provision of car-parking in the 21st century.

The Leisure Age

An astonishing rise in car ownership occurred alongside the shortening of the working week and an increase in paid holiday time. As well as exotic travel, people began to look for varied forms of entertainment and leisure activities closer to home.

In 1946, when the Government was urging development of sports facilities and other help for youth organisations, the Borough Council acquired 27 acres from Broadlands to develop into the Romsey Sports Centre. This comprised the playing field previously used by Osborne House School as well as allotments and the old recreation ground. At the same time the tennis courts and the bowling greens in the Memorial Park were renovated. Well-established youth movements including Scouts, Guides, Boys' and Girls' Brigades, Army and Sea Cadets received support with projects such as new headquarters.

The old swimming pool by the Crosfield Hall was covered in as an indoor facility, but this was a short extension to its life and it closed some fifty years after it had opened; it became a car park. The Romsey Rapids, a new leisure complex, which included a swimming pool, was opened at the Romsey Sports Centre. Hunts Farm at Timsbury provided further sports facilities towards the end of the 20th century.

Many locations around Romsey have become popular venues for a whole range of activities. The Crosfield Hall, the town hall, the Abbey and King John's House (now run by a Trust) are among many places used for talks and meetings, music, fund-raising and exhibitions.

The Romsey Amateur Operatic and Dramatic Society (RAODS) found its own home. The *Plaza* cinema had closed and had been sold in 1980 as a Bingo Hall. Two years later and it was for sale again. This time it saw the beginning of a new and successful life. RAODS, founded in 1934, purchased the building and have improved it enormously over the years. Romsey Art Group also found its own centre. This is the old chapel-of-ease at Lee, now the Lee Gallery. High standard art exhibitions are now a regular feature in this building.

In the 1970s, a new surge of interest in the archaeology and history of the locality resulted in the formation of two organisations. One was a professional archaeological unit, largely funded by Test Valley Borough Council and known first as Test Valley Archaeological Committee (TVAC) and later as Test Valley Archaeological Trust (TVAT). The other was the group responsible for this and many earlier publications - the Lower Test Valley Archaeological Study Group (LTVAS). After sharing a room at TVAT's long held offices at Orchard House, the LTVAS Group had, by the end of the century, found splendid accommodation in the basement of Romsey town hall and was going from strength to strength.

The town is rich in numerous other groups providing for horticulturalists, sports enthusiasts, artists, craftspeople, searchers after knowledge, and fund-raising groups. Disabilities and all ages are catered for, and there is particular support for young people, who have a 'drop-in' centre in Bell Street. *The Romsey Advertiser*, which celebrated its 100th birthday in 1996, is the source of information about events organised by these groups, as well as keeping its readers aware of local news.

Besides these on-going activities, there have been special celebrations, which people have supported with enthusiasm. There was a 'Strolling Pageant' as Romsey's contribution to the 1951 Festival of Britain. Then, in 1957, the Queen and Duke of Edinburgh, who had spent part of their honeymoon at Broadlands some 10 years earlier, came to Romsey for the 350th anniversary of the granting of the borough charter.

Other more regular events punctuated the Romsey calendar over the century and still do. The Romsey Agricultural and Horse Show Society hosts the Romsey Show in Broadlands Park, an event that draws participants and visitors from a very wide area. Annual carnivals also attract people to the town, with Romsey's Old Cadets Band a highly popular feature. For many years the Brewery gave splendid support to the carnival. It entered its own float, loaned vehicles to other organisations, and allowed the floats to assemble in the Brewery yard.

By the end of the 20th century there were two carnivals each year, one in the summer and one near Christmas. The Christmas carnival has helped to put Romsey on the map as a Christmas attraction. A new custom has created a special 'Christmas Shopping Event', when - usually on the second Friday in December - the town centre is closed to traffic and turned into one great open market with street entertainment.

Moody's Old Gunshop

The shops stay open until 9pm and Father Christmas makes a dramatic appearance on the roof of one of the Market Place buildings.

More recently, July has seen the introduction of an annual Beggars' Fair and a triennial Arts Festival. Both these events include a wide range of people, interests and locations throughout Romsey. The attractions of the town and the surrounding area have been brought to a much wider audience since the 1983 opening of the Tourist Information Centre, which transferred in the summer of 2000 to a new Heritage and Visitor Centre in Church Street, in premises known locally as Moody's old gunshop.

Broadlands
In 1979 Lord Louis Mountbatten decided to open his Broadlands home to the public. The official opening was carried out by Prince Charles. The Royal Family were regular visitors to Romsey when Lord and Lady Mountbatten were in residence. The house had been renovated after the war, and the Victorian north wing demolished, making it less expensive to maintain, and returning the house to the classical Palladian shape of Browns' original design.

Just a few months later, the town and the entire country were shocked and saddened by Lord Mountbatten's assassination. After a brief closure, the house re-opened to the public with a special exhibition about his life. Poignantly, Lord Mountbatten's gesture in opening the house to the public, and the tragedy of his death, brought a new wave of tourism to the town itself.

In 1981 the Prince of Wales brought his young bride, Princess Diana, to Broadlands for part of their honeymoon. Sadly, this was another story with a Broadlands link that was destined to end in tragedy.

Local Government

Before his death Lord Mountbatten had been concerned about the effect on Romsey of the Parliamentary act that led to the re-organisation of local government in 1974. Until then the Romsey & Stockbridge Rural District Council had operated from Duttons Road, while the Romsey Borough Council had its centre in Romsey town hall with some additional outside space. The Borough Council Proceedings of March 1946 recorded the need to reorganise office accommodation at the town hall to save the rent of No 2 Abbey Water (but with no indication of its use).

A month later, it was agreed that renovations to the town hall were urgent - the roof itself and the ceilings and floor of the Assembly Hall (on the ground floor) were in a bad state. At that time it was necessary to rent a room in the yard at the rear of the town hall for staff cycles. The Assembly Hall was also to be converted into an office and a Public Library. The tenders for this last work were accepted two and a half years later in 1948.

Then came the great changes of 1974, when the new Test Valley Borough Council came into being, absorbing both Romsey Infra and Romsey Extra which each became a parish council. Romsey town's long history as an independent borough was at an end. But the Council was only known as Romsey Parish Council, in the year immediately preceding the official change-over date. The Council then resolved to adopt town status, thereafter to be known as the Romsey Town Council. With Lord Mountbatten's support, the chairman and vice-chairman were to be known as Town Mayor and Deputy

Town Mayor.   But most of the property owned by the old Borough Council passed to the new Test Valley Borough Council, which continued to use Romsey town hall until an extension had been built to the Duttons Road offices.

Then, by 1975, the town hall was seemingly redundant.   The Library which had been in the main downstairs room had moved to the old school in Station Road in 1968 and the Magistrates Court had a new building in Church Street.   There were ideas of demolishing the town hall and replacing it with shops or perhaps a museum.

Eventually it was decided that the Romsey Town Council needed offices, and there was need for a prestigious meeting place in the centre of the town.   So the town had to buy back the property from the TVBC.   At first, it was thought that the best way to finance the property was to make the building a Community Centre, and in 1982 a public meeting was called to discuss the project.

By this time the building was in serious need of repair and re-organisation of the interior was essential.   The first basic renovation took place in 1980-81 and in 1983 the Community Association arranged with the Town Council to manage the leasing for 28 years of the available parts of the hall. Notification to terminate that lease was given in December 1984 and in 1985 it was decided that the Town Council should be responsible for the total building including any leasing arrangements.   The renovation was completed in 1986, and Romsey town hall is now a venue for civil marriages as well as being available for meetings, exhibitions and special events.

Health and Welfare
There was a general welcome for the National Health Service when it came into being in 1948, and the expectations of the local community have been well served by medical provisions within the town.   At first there was concern about the future of Romsey Hospital in the context of the new National Health Service, but the problem was resolved.   To quote Dr Peter Johnson:
> 'Romsey weathered this storm, sometimes keeping its head down and lying low and sometimes standing up

238

and trumpeting politely its defiant intention to keep going'.

There was a very successful hospital appeal in 1978 to enable the hospital to provide more and improved services, and in 1998 another appeal was launched for further extensions, which in 2000 are already being built.

The growth in population led to an increase in medical support within the town. Established surgeries at Abbey Meads and Alma Road became bigger and more stream-lined, and then supported a completely new surgery, Nightingale Surgery, opened in Great Well Drive off Cupernham Lane in 1983. The growth in population also made another and sadder provision necessary. In 1983, Woodley Cemetery opened.

Care of the poor also underwent a change. In April 1948, the headline of *The Romsey Advertiser* declared 'A Memorable Last Meeting - Health Committee Take Over Next Month'. The last meeting was of the Guardians and Relieving Officers of the Poor. A new more central administration was taking over, and the old workhouse was to become a 'Hostel for the aged'. Care of all in need was henceforth to fall within the umbrella of the newly designated 'Welfare State'. The upkeep of the poor would no longer fall on their relatives, and the old idea of settlement and removal was swept away.

Education
The temporary buildings that housed Romsey's secondary school behind Plaza Parade lasted some 25 years until the post-war reorganisation of education, planned in 1938 and executed under the Butler 1944 Education Act. This raised the school leaving age to 15, later extended to 16, and greatly enlarged the curriculum. The first development in Romsey was the opening of the purpose-built secondary school at Priestlands, now called The Romsey School. Many more pupils now undertake further education.

Once this secondary school had opened, it was possible to begin to release the bottleneck in the town's educational framework. The Church of England Boys' School in Station Road was closed in 1957. The building was occupied for a short while by the Civil Defence Unit and then became the Romsey branch of the County Library. The Church of England Girls' and Infants' School near the Abbey became the Romsey Abbey Primary School.

A Romsey County Junior School, with Mr Mercer as the first headteacher, was established in the former buildings of Romsey Council Secondary School, behind Plaza Parade. It catered for juniors of both sexes and used the old huts until a new building was put up a few years later. Two classrooms in the new building were allocated to older infants, so some of the old huts stayed in use. The younger infants of this school remained at the old British School buildings in The Hundred until 1974.

More new schools were required as housing developments grew. A school for 5-11 year olds was opened at Cupernham in 1968 with a separate Infants' building on the same campus a few years later. A new secondary school, Mountbatten School, opened in 1969 and this was followed by Halterworth Primary School and a new Romsey Junior School on a site off Mercer Way. Once this last school was open, Romsey Infants' School finally took over the building behind Plaza Parade. The old 'British School' property was then sold. For a while it was occupied by a language school before being converted into private houses called English Court.

There was much discussion between the wars about the necessity for nursery education for the under-fives. In the 1950s and 1960s pre-school groups were started privately, providing varied standards of activities and care. In 1974 a nursery unit was opened in one of the huts remaining in the grounds of Romsey Infants' School behind Plaza Parade. Eventually, a more universal provision was made by introducing entry to all Hampshire infant schools in the September of the year in which a child reached its fifth birthday.

The other end of the educational spectrum also expanded, and secondary schools opened during the evenings for adult education. A wide range of subjects, practical and academic, gradually included self-improvement and keep-fit sessions. A 'University of the Third Age', or U3A, was formed in Romsey, and receives considerable support. The 16-18 year olds, however, have to travel out of Romsey for sixth form education.

Private Schools

Osborne House, commandeered by the Council during the war after the end of its life as a private school, was still in use until the new secondary school opened at Priestlands in 1957. Osborne House was then demolished in 1964, leaving a car parking space for some time. The Abbey Walk set of shops has now been built on the site.

In the post-war years, the one-time St Joseph's Orphanage developed into a very popular fee-paying girls' school. This school prospered as La Sagesse Convent School. Over the years new buildings were added and a preparatory section for boys was maintained. It served girls from Romsey and the surrounding area for many years, finally closing in 1995, partly because the buildings for the senior girls were said to be unsafe. The governors of Embley Park School had been considering starting a junior school, and leased the Convent junior school building to provide short term accommodation until a new junior school was built at Embley Park in the year 2000. Planning permission was then given for a nursing home to be built in the convent grounds - another transformation of this historic site for the 21st century.

In 1977 Montfort College Seminary closed in Romsey, and moved to London. The College authorities owned a considerable acreage of land at Halterworth, which they had farmed. In the decades after the Second World War much of this land was sold for housing and for Halterworth School. Finally, Montfort House itself was converted into flats and offices.

Just as Embley Park School near Wellow was adapted from the Nightingale family home, so Stroud Preparatory School was developed at Highwood House, well known to earlier generations as the home of Mrs Florence Suckling. It opened in 1953. Another of the old rural manor houses, Stanbridge Earls, also became a school, which in recent years has gained widespread recognition for helping children with learning problems such as dyslexia.

Romsey Churches

The dissenting churches maintained a strong presence in Romsey throughout the 20th century. Some smaller groups meet in hired venues, while the distinctive buildings of the Baptists, Methodists and Congregationalists have become established landmarks in the town, their members participating in many local events. The two groups of Methodists having united in 1932, the old Middlebridge Street chapel is now occupied by the Elim Pentecostal Church under its more recent name of the Romsey Christian Centre. In 1972, the Congregationalists merged with the English Presbyterians, transforming their 'Church by the Arch' into the United Reformed Church. Meanwhile, in 1961, Romsey became a separate Roman Catholic parish, having hitherto been part of St Boniface's in Shirley, Southampton.

It was Romsey Abbey, though, that continued to play the central role in the town's life, its tower frequently flying a flag to reflect the town's reactions to a range of joyous and tragic events. With regular civic services, some interdenominational services and special musical events, the church opened its doors to a wide congregation. Schools presented concerts and carol services, and the restored Walker organ featured on many occasions. 'Music in Romsey' became a regular and popular attraction.

There have also been outstanding special days at the Abbey, many relating to aspects of life at Broadlands. In 1946 and 1960 Lord Mountbatten's daughters were married there. Decades later, a more sombre gathering witnessed his funeral. His plain tombstone is in the south transept.

The tombstones in the churchyard, or North Garth, were removed in the late 1940s and laid flat as paving slabs, and the grass was levelled. In the 1960s the building to the west that had been the old town hall from 1820-66 was pulled down and the present church rooms built in its place. Several archaeological excavations yielded more of the Abbey's secrets, published in a monograph of 1996.

When Smiths of Derby were called back to overhaul the Abbey clock in 1973, they were assisted this time by Simon Kersey, grandson of the same Frederick Walter Kersey who had helped in 1924. Simon Kersey still attends to the clock if it stops or needs altering.

1994 was a momentous year. It marked the 450th anniversary of the purchase of Romsey Abbey as the town's parish church. A specially written pageant was presented in the nave, and a commemorative stone in the floor of the choir paid lasting tribute to the four men who had negotiated the purchase.

The Millennium
The end of the 1900s came and went with less drama than was expected by many. The year 2000AD (or 2000CE for 'Common Era', as preferred by some) was recognised as a significant moment in the western calendar, and marked in Romsey, to quote *The Romsey Advertiser*, 'with a massive street party that blended the sacred with the secular'. There was an ecumenical millennium service in the Abbey, a torchlight procession and dancing in the Market Place until just before midnight. Then the vicar read a prayer, the clock chimed, the bells rang and the fireworks exploded.

All was in sharp contrast with New Year's Eve in 1900. That year it fell on a Sunday, but the vicar was ill so there was no service in the Abbey. The Nonconformists held a united service in the Baptist Chapel but *The Romsey Advertiser* commented that 'few people were abroad at midnight'.

The dawn of the year 2000 was a family celebration and the thousand or so people who packed the Market Place and surrounding streets were good humoured and well-behaved. There was considerable enjoyment of the fact that town councillors were manning the public conveniences and the town hall, whose regular attendants had been given a bank holiday.

~~~~~~~~~~~~~~~

The Lower Test Valley Archaeological Study Group (LTVAS), founded in 1973 to study the archaeology and local history of the area, had long decided that this new history of Romsey would be its members' contribution to the Millennium. The Council Chamber of the town hall was booked for the launch on Monday, 9th October 2000.

APPENDIX: MONEY and WAGES GUIDE

£ s. d.

Old money, as opposed to the present metric money, was most popularly referred to as 'Pounds, shillings and pence'.

- **Pounds**, as now, were identified by the £ sign. This sign comes from a capital L with a line struck through thus Ŀ to show that it is an abbreviation for *Libra*, Latin for a pound.
- **Shillings** were abbreviated as 's', though this actually came from *solidus*, the Latin for shilling.
- **Pence** were shown as 'd' from the Latin for a penny, which was *denarius*.

Pennies

    12d = 1 shilling
    240d = £1

- **Half-penny**: A penny could be divided into halves, each known as a half-penny or ha'penny (½d)
- **Farthing**: A penny could also be divided into quarters, each known as a farthing (¼d); three farthings would be represented as ¾d.

Shillings

    20s = £1
    21s = 1 guinea (£1 1s 0d)
    42s = 2 guineas (£2 2s 0d) and so forth

NOTE: Sums of shillings and pence might be written as 2s 6d or 2/6. The latter style was particularly popular in shop displays.

Special Historic Denominations

- **Mark**: A mark was set at 13s 4d and half a mark at 6s 8d.
- **Mancus**: Old English money of account worth 30 pence
- **Groat**: A groat was a silver coin worth four pence

NB: The mark and mancus were not coins but values used as 'money of account'. In respect of coinage, there were many changes within the old money system over the centuries.

Some equivalent sums of money

Old Money	6d	1s 0d	2s 6d	3s 4d	6s 8d	10s 0d	13s 4d	15s 0d
New Money	2½p	5p	12½p	16-17p	37p	50p	66-67p	75p

Wages and Prices

There is little advantage in making a direct conversion into modern money without some idea of wages and the purchasing power of money at any one time. Here are some guidelines to money values in various centuries. As well as showing the changing level of wages, the following illustrations show that some goods were once more expensive in real terms than today, while others have become cheaper.

- An ordinary workman in the medieval period would probably earn 2d-6d a day, according to skills, with a reduction if food was supplied. He might be employed for only a few weeks at a time, and then have to find other work.
- Wages were fixed in Winchester in 1563.
  - A master workman - carpenter, plumber, joiner and such like - could earn 9d a day in winter and 10d a day in summer up to a maximum of 5s 0d a week.
  - A common workman could have 7d or 8d a day with a maximum of 4s 0d a week.

Note: 4d a day was deducted if food was provided.

  - Women servants under 18 years were to be paid no wages but given meat, drink and necessary apparel. Above that age the 'common sort' of woman servant was to have 16s 0d a year and the best 20s 0d [£1] a year.
- In Romsey in 1594, 10s 0d would have bought 3 geese, a gander, 3 ducks, a mallard, 16 hens and 3 cocks, but only about 5 yards of a plain linen material called Holland or 1½ yards of taffeta. In view of the comparatively high cost of material, it is not surprising that clothes formed important and much appreciated bequests in Tudor wills.
- In 1838 a poor Romsey labourer was struggling on 9s 0d a week, plus 2s 0d a week being earned by his eldest 14 year old son. He was paying 2s 0d rent a week. The cost to the local workhouse for the whole family of 7 was calculated to be 18s 0d a week.
- In the 1920s/1930s a long-serving employee of Strong & Co. Ltd, the Romsey brewery, might be earning £2 a week.
- Between the wars there was a High Street firm known as 'Fifty Shilling Tailors', set up to sell suits at 50s 0d (£2 50p) or less.

Acknowledgements

The authors and contributors wish to thank fellow LTVAS members who have supported the production of this book, particularly Jeff Hawksley for map-drawing and Tony Burbridge for computer work.

Further thanks are due to

Sue Collins for reading the draft as an 'outsider'
Reg Leeman, director of Wills Nursery, for his recollections
Mary Harris for advice about the Swing Riots
Andy Russel for his archaeological advice
Readers of *The Romsey Advertiser* for supplying information

References and Sources

Detailed references have not been included in this book, but are available from LTVAS (Town Hall, Market Place, Romsey).

Principal Sources other than LTVAS Resources

Hampshire Record Office
Ordnance Survey Maps of Romsey
Public Record Office
Sites & Monuments Records for the Test Valley
Southampton Record Office
Test Valley Archaeological Trust
The Romsey Advertiser

Select Bibliography

We particularly recommend the following LTVAS books, which add detail to matters only touched upon in this general history:

After the Rhinoceros: a Story of Romsey's Railways
Mills & Waterways of Romsey
Romsey Schools, 900-1940
Sir W.P. (The story of Sir William Petty)

Coates, R.	The Place-Names of Hampshire	Batsford, 1989
Coldicott, D.K.	Hampshire Nunneries	Phillimore, 1989
Collier, C.	Romsey Minster in Saxon Times	HFC Proceedings, 1991
Harrison, W.	Description of England	1587
Himsworth, S. (Editor)	Winchester College Muniments Volume II	Phillimore, 1984
Latham, Dr J.	Unpublished History of Romsey	BL Mss 26774-26780
Liveing, H.G.D.	Records of Romsey Abbey	Warren & Son Ltd, Winchester, 1912
Merrick, P.	The Administration of Ulnage & Subsidy on Woollen Cloth, 1394-1485 with a case study of Hampshire	MPhil Thesis, 1997
Morris, J. (ed.)	Domesday Book, Hampshire	Phillimore, 1982
Scott, I.	Romsey Abbey: Report on Excavations, 1973-91	Hampshire Field Club & TVAT, 1996
Walker, J.	Romsey Abbey through the Centuries	Pendragon Press, 1993
Page. W. (Ed.)	VCH: Hampshire & IOW	London, 1911
Whiteman, A. (editor)	The Compton Census of 1676: A Critical Edition	OUP, 1986

INDEX

Black Death, 42, 43, 44, 45, 48, 60, 66
blacksmiths, 20
Blake, John Denner (diarist), 145
Borough boundary change, 158
Borough changes, 180
Borough Corporation Picnic, 163
Borough of Romsey, 101, 102, 104
    charter of incorporation, 101, 102, 103, 110, 111, 235
    Housing Committee, 192
    Municipal Charities, 192
    parish council, 237
botanical evidence, 15
Botley Road, 40, 143, 146, 186, 194, 200, 212, 213, 224, 225
Bowman's Farm, 11
Braishfield Chantry, 30
Braishfield, Nicholas de, 30
Braishfield, Nicholas de, 46, 53
bread prices, 99, 115, 130
brewing (see also Strong & Co. Ltd), 126, 137, 145, 156
    inns and taverns, 126
brick, use of, 91, 113, 114, 132, 143, 148, 157, 193
Bricklayers Arms, The, 132
bridges, 103, 123, 128
British Legion, 190
Broad Bridge, 26, 61, 78, 91
Broadlands (see also Ashley, Fleming, Cowper-Temple, Mountbatten, Palmerston, St Barbe), 10, 12, 32, 37, 38, 53, 84, 91, 101, 123, 132, 143, 146, 148, 153, 160, 164, 168, 170, 185, 186, 194, 196, 205, 215, 219, 234, 235, 236, 237
Broadwater Road, 15, 225, 226, 233
Broom Hill, 11
Buckell, Miss Fanny, 179, 188
Budds Lane, 36, 180, 207, 230

bull-baiting, 122
bus station, 233
butchers, 34, 59, 61, 68, 111, 122, 130, 170, 199, 231
    Stares, Walter, 189
Bypass, 197, 219, 233

canal, Andover-Redbridge, 129, 141, 143, 218
car ownership, 233
Caravans, Country Life, 200, 218, 230
carnival, 163, 236
Casbrook Common, 15
cemetery, 75
    Abbey churchyard, 146
    Botley Road, 146, 172, 215
    Burial Board, 146
    Woodley, 239
Chambers Avenue, 224
chapels-of-ease, 144
Cherville Street, 33, 35, 41, 61, 76, 80, 121, 128, 135, 151, 158, 168, 169, 195, 226
Christmas Shopping Event, 236
Church Court, 157, 193
Church Lane, 148
Church Street, 22, 33, 35, 39, 40, 54, 57, 59, 61, 66, 73, 106, 107, 108, 133, 145, 147, 149, 159, 160, 168, 178, 183, 189, 198, 211, 212, 229, 238
Churchgate Street, 33, 35, 40
Civil Defence, 240
Civil War, 103, 104, 105, 106
cloth
    customs duties, 54
    ulnage, 55, 57, 58, 59, 60
cloth dealers, 55, 57, 59, 114
    Italian merchants, 58, 64, 73
cloth-finishing, 41, 42, 55, 59, 99, 108, 114, 115, 123
    dyeing, 42, 54, 57, 58, 116

248

fulling, 37, 41, 42, 54, 57, 58, 73, 79, 80, 87, 88, 130
cloth-finishing suppliers, 35, 57
cloth-finishing supplies, 57, 60
cloth-making, 42, 103, 108, 117
cloths of assise, 57, 59
coaching trade, 126, 130, 136, 142, 143
Cobbett, William, 135, 141
Cock Close, 192
cock-fighting, 122
coffin, lead, 19
common fields, names of, 37
commons and common rights, 134
Cooper's engineering works, 172, 183, 199
Corn Exchange, 145, 146, 155, 160, 204, 211
Cornmarket, 145, 233
county councillor, 159
Court Leet, 121, 128
court records, names in, 37, 38, 67, 68
Cowper-Temple, Rt Hon. William of Broadlands, 149, 155
craftsmen, 34, 87, 92, 114, 202
craftsmen, names of, 42, 173
Crampmoor, 144
Crescent, The, 176
Crosfield Hall, 205, 220, 234
Crosfield, Mr and Mrs J.J., 205
Cross Keys, 164
Cupernham, 10, 12, 16, 17, 22, 37, 40, 67, 76, 86, 125, 176, 192, 194, 219, 226
Cupernham Lane, 37, 135, 239
curfew bell, 88

Danes, 23
Dolphin, 128, 228
Domesday Book, 23, 24, 25, 28, 34, 43, 50

Duttons Road, 143, 184, 193, 207, 224, 237, 238

Edgar, King, 22, 23, 29, 32, 47
Edington, 45
Edington, Bishop William of, 45
education, 118, 133, 147, 178, 192
  adult education, 240
  British and Foreign Bible Society, 148
  Cowper-Temple clause, 155
  Education Acts, 139, 146, 149, 155, 178, 239
education, reorganisation of, 239
Edward I, King, 28, 32
Edward the Elder, King, 21
Edwina Mountbatten House, 173
Elcombe's (seed merchants), 188
electricity, 196
  W. Hampshire Electricity Co., 196
Elim Pentecostal Church, 242
Elite cinema, 185, 204
  cinema pianist, 204
Ely, Thomas & Sons (ironmongers), 198
Embley, 20, 25, 34, 63, 146, 199, 205
enclosure roads, 134
Eny Lane, 32
Eny Street, 32, 61, 62
Ethulwulf, King, 20

Fair Field, 185
fairs, 31, 110, 114, 145, 159, 168, 185
  Beggars' Fair, 236
fire service, 147
Fire Service, 213
Fishlake, 157, 161, 175, 205
Fishlake Arch, 184
Fishlake Meadows, 227

252